The
Spirit
of
Wisdom and Revelation

WATCHMAN NEE

Translated from the Chinese

Christian Fellowship Publishers, Inc.
New York

Available from the Publishers at:

11515 Allecingie Parkway
Richmond, Virginia 23235

TRANSLATOR'S PREFACE

How absolutely vital it is for Christians to understand and to experience the prayer of Paul: "The God of our Lord Jesus Christ, the Father of glory, may give unto you a spirit of wisdom and revelation in the knowledge of him" (Eph. 1.17). It means life or death to our Christian life. There is no way of knowing God and His eternal will except through revelation. Neither is there any means of knowing Christ other than by the revelation of the Holy Spirit. Revelation alone imparts to us spiritual realities.

In this new volume now available in English, Watchman Nee opens up this subject of the spirit of wisdom and revelation by explaining Paul's famous prayer which he offered up on behalf of the Ephesian believers. How necessary it is, the author points out, for us to have the spirit of wisdom and revelation if we are to know God at all. He then proceeds to enlighten us as to some of the spiritual realities which must indeed come through revelation, such as Christ the Rock of the church, Christ the great "I Am," the Christ in glory—together with the four ministers of the New Testament. The author concludes by exhorting the church to work with God in bringing in the kingdom of the heavens.

As we are approaching the end of this age, we will come to see that those things which are to be shaken shall be removed and only those things which are not to be shaken shall remain. May we therefore seek for things unshakable which come through the spirit of wisdom and revelation.

CONTENTS

This volume consists of messages delivered by the author over an extended period of anointed ministry of God's word. Because of the relatedness of their content, they are now being translated and published in English as a single volume.

Scripture quotations are from the
American Standard Version of the Bible
(1901), unless otherwise indicated.

1 | The Spirit of Wisdom and Revelation

For this cause I also, having heard of the faith in the Lord Jesus which is among you, and the love which ye show toward all the saints, cease not to give thanks for you, making mention of you in my prayers; that the God of our Lord Jesus Christ, the Father of glory, may give unto you a spirit of wisdom and revelation in the knowledge of him; having the eyes of your heart enlightened, that ye may know what is the hope of his calling, what the riches of the glory of his inheritance in the saints, and what the exceeding greatness of his power to us-ward who believe, according to that working of the strength of his might which he wrought in Christ, when he raised him from the dead, and made him to sit at his right hand in the heavenly places, far above all rule, and authority, and power, and dominion, and every name that is named, not only in this world, but also in that which is to come: and he put all things in subjection under his feet, and gave him to be head over all things to the church, which is his body, the fulness of him that filleth all in all. (Eph. 1.15-23)

A Prayer for Revelation

As we begin to know God, His purpose ordained in eternity, and His work throughout the ages, we shall increasingly realize how many-sided, lofty, and special are the insights which God reveals to us in Paul's Letter to the Ephesians. We cannot fail to notice this one thing, that in this letter God causes Paul to record the fact that he prays two prayers: the one prayer as mentioned in chapter 1, and the other prayer that is mentioned in chapter 3. The first prayer is foundational whereas the second prayer is for building up. In the first chapter Paul's prayer is for us to know our relationship with the Lord, while in the third chapter his prayer is for us to know our relationship with the church as well as that with the Lord. We will at present only concentrate on the prayer found in the first chapter of Ephesians.

Paul begins his prayer with these words: "that the God of our Lord Jesus Christ, the Father of glory, may give unto you a spirit of wisdom and revelation." Why does he long for the Ephesian believers to have the spirit of wisdom and revelation? Quite simply, that they may know the following three things:

(1) "The knowledge of him" (v.17)—This is knowing God himself.

(2) "That ye may know what is the hope of his calling, what the riches of the glory of his inheritance in the saints" (v.18)—This points to the eternal plan of God and its fulfillment. The gracious calling of God is a calling of us to be His sons, and these sons shall be His inheritance. The call of God was preordained

before the foundation of the world, whereas the riches of the glory of His inheritance in the saints will be realized in the eternity to come. In eternity past God has a will, and in eternity to come He will have a possession. The putting together of these two facts reveals the eternal purpose and plan of God. So that what Paul wants us to know is God's eternal plan.

And (3) "What the exceeding greatness of his power to us-ward who believe" (v.19)—This statement shows us what power God will use today to achieve His purpose and to accomplish His plan. Hence it deals especially with our relationship to Him today and also our relationship to His purpose in eternity.

These things we need to consider and to have revelation about before God. Let us take up each of these three matters more fully.

Truly Know God

We have seen that Paul asks God to grant us the spirit of wisdom and revelation that we may know several things. And the very first of these is "the knowledge of him"—that is to say, that we may know God. How marvelous that we may indeed know the God of the universe!

When Paul passed through Athens he saw an altar with this inscription: "To An Unknown God" (Acts 17.23). In the minds of the Athenians at that time God was considered as being unknowable—that they could not know Him by the searching of their mind. Even with their many philosophies, they still could not understand Him. The Athenians had their imaginations and theories, but they had no way to know the one true God. Their situation was not any different from that of today with people who may say that there is a God yet who do not really know Him. On the verge of His departure from earth the Lord Jesus boldly declared these words: "This is life eternal, that they should know thee the only true God, and him whom thou didst send, even Jesus Christ" (John 17.3). Jesus shows us what eternal life is: simply put, eternal life is knowing God. Now the saints in Ephesus, as is made quite clear in the Scriptures, had already known God. No one could argue that they did not. They had actually known Him and already were in possession of eternal life. Yet we must note that Paul still prayed a prayer for them in which he asked God to give to them "a spirit of wisdom and revelation in the knowledge of him." From all this we may easily conclude that while the Athenians plainly did not know God at all, even so, Christians who have eternal life and who have thus already known God need nonetheless to know Him more.

When we have believed in the Lord for several years—or even in the case of having just first believed in Him—we cannot say we do not know God, for we do know Him. Yet many times we find ourselves still needing the support of our mind or feeling to help us onward. We have a little knowledge of God, but in addition to such little knowledge we believe we need the help of many ideas; for without these ideas we feel as if our little knowledge of God is undependable and insufficient. With the result that we often require the assistance of these ideas to maintain our Christian life. Without such mental aids we find it hard to convince ourselves of the correctness in reason and doctrine for us to press on. And furthermore, many times we seek for warm, joyful or stirring feelings as additional help to our on-going walk with the Lord.

The day may come, however, when God gives us the spirit of wisdom and revelation in revealing himself in a fresh, special, and deeper way to us, so that we may declare that we now truly know Him. At that time we will boldly assert: "I now understand and see clearly. I no longer need the help of either ideas or feelings. I now truly know God."

Perhaps some of you cannot fully comprehend what has just been said. Let us therefore illustrate this point with one or two examples. Once a Christian testified with the following words: "I have believed the Lord for 22 years. During the first two of those years I tried my best to believe. If I was asked whether I was saved, I was truly saved. None could say I was not saved, for I knew I was. I also knew I had eternal life. Yet I had a problem. For whenever I was asked whether I believed in God, I answered that I indeed believed in Him, but I found myself saying the word "believe" most emphatically as though I were forcing myself to believe—as though I consciously had to lay hold of myself lest I might then and there stop being a Christian. And hence my believing in the Lord Jesus required my own effort to believe. Did I believe in God? I did. Did I know Him? I honestly did not know if I knew Him. I needed the aid of many reasons and doctrines to protect my faith. I felt safe and could even talk with others so long as my reasons were logical and my doctrines were sound. I needed mental assistance in my Christian life. But today I can testify that I am no longer that way. Today I can say I know my God. I no longer require mental aids for support: I do not need outward evidence to protect my inward faith.''

What this Christian has said is what truly knowing God is. Such knowledge comes from revelation: not because the doctrine is good, but because you know it inwardly by revelation. It is different from the kind of knowing which you had immediately subsequent to the moment of being saved. For at that time you felt your knowledge had to be handled with the utmost of care out of fear lest it be damaged in some way or even be lost. For many people, their faith in the Lord Jesus is dependent continually upon their having to walk carefully: they are always afraid of hearing anything different which might overturn their knowledge of God. But one day God gives them revelation. They begin to know Him inwardly because they have truly seen Him; and all problems are solved.

Let me say that were you truly to know God, then neither the faith of the entire world would help you believe nor would the unbelief of the entire world shake loose your faith. Perhaps other people may assert so convincingly that the Bible is totally false and their reasons for unbelief may seem to be far more overwhelming than all the reasons for believing; yet no matter how many reasons they may marshal before you, your faith will not be shaken. Instead, you can now speak ever so boldly: ''I have come to know God inwardly. My knowledge is deeper than thought and is deeper than feeling. I today inwardly understand; and therefore nothing from outside can sway me.''

This that we have been discussing is indeed a big problem for believers. Many Christians live too much by feeling. If they feel joyful and happy today they will say God has truly blessed them. If, however, they feel cold and flat today they each will almost be heard to say, How can I know where God is? Thus many Christians lean upon their feeling; and as soon as their feeling is missing, they waver. This proves that they do not really know the Lord. How the children of God need to be brought by the Lord to the place where feeling cold or warm, flat or stirred, presents no problem because they have known God with a knowledge which is deeper than any feeling. In spite of varied sensations outwardly—whether of joy or pain—they inwardly know. And only such persons as these can stand against all shakings. Such people alone will be used by God.

There was once a brother who, not long after he had believed in the Lord, was confronted by another person who told him that there were errors in the Bible. He was so exasperated that he nearly cried. Here was one who believed the Bible to be true; how then could there be any error? Nevertheless, this other man, in pointing out several places in the Bible, hinted that these were in error. So that the brother was really afraid. Shaken as he was, he thought: What can I do if these *are* real errors? Whereupon he laid this matter before an elderly sister, for he reckoned that since this sister loved the Lord and loved the Bible so much she certainly would be agitated if she realized there were these errors in the Bible. The strange thing was, however, that after this sister heard him out, she was calm as could be. Her reply to his presentation was: This is no problem. The brother now mused within himself with these words: Even if this creates no problem for her, it most assuredly poses a great problem for me! He therefore asked the sister to explain to him these questionable places in the Bible. Yet all she said was, that knowing God did not depend on the solving of these questions! To which the brother inwardly responded by thinking in his heart: These problems might not require any solution for an elderly person like you, but it is impossible for a young man with an active mind like mine to overlook them. With the result that this brother spent an entire year searching the Scriptures with regard to these questions. Upon finding out the evidence that the Bible passages in question were correct and not in error, the heavy burden upon his heart dropped away like a stone that is lifted from someone's shoulder. Actually, though, if this brother had truly known God he would not have needed to worry for a whole year.

If we truly know God we will not carry in our hearts such a heavy burden nor be disturbed even though there may come our way many more questions. People may attempt to prove this or that thing, but we Christians can prove one very important thing—that God is indeed God and that we know Him who is so real. And by knowing Him, all problems are solved. Such knowledge does not rely on how logical are the reasons or how clear the doctrines; it relies only on revelation. How such revelation is absolutely necessary. We must ask God to give us the spirit of revelation so that we may really know Him. And knowledge such as this is the foundation of a believer and is of utmost importance.

Know God's Call and God's Inheritance

God wants us not only to know Him but also to know what His calling and what His inheritance in the saints are. In other words, He wants us to know what He has been doing and continues to do from eternity to eternity—in short, what His eternal plan and purpose are.

We should realize that the Letter to the Ephesians —in showing us what the eternal plan of God is— deals with this matter from eternity to eternity. In mentioning God's call, His inheritance in the saints, and His power towards us who believe, Paul intends to tell us that for us truly to know God's eternal plan and what He is doing from eternity to eternity we need to see the relationship between God's eternal plan on the one hand and His calling us, His inheritance in us, and His power towards us on the other. Only with this understanding will we not approach the eternal plan of God in an abstract way nor reckon His eternal plan as insignificant. Let us see that this eternal plan of God is closely related to each one of us. When we talk about it, should we treat it as something intangible and incomprehensible? Not at all.

For it has very much to do with us practically; it is directly related to His calling us, to His inheritance in us, and to His power towards us. And these are all very personal matters to us in a practical way.

Let us consider God's calling and inheritance first before proceeding on to discuss God's power towards those who believe.

As regards our calling, read again Paul's prayer on this aspect: ". . . having the eyes of your heart enlightened, that ye may know what is the hope of his calling" (v.18). We may wonder if many Christians know there is a hope before them. Yet the hope of many who do, turns out to be merely heaven. Thank God, there *is* the hope of heaven. But heaven is not the purpose of God's calling us, nor is it our hope of His gracious call. What, then, is this gracious call? "Even as he chose us in him before the foundation of the world, that we should be holy and without blemish before him in love" (1.4). This is God's call. He calls us to be like Him—stated positively, to be holy; stated negatively, to be without blemish.

Oh how great is this gracious calling! If you have never fallen or been weak, you may not appreciate the uniqueness of this calling. But in case you know somewhat of the depth of your weakness and uselessness, how dearly you will embrace it. You will say: "Thank God, You call me to be holy, You call me to be blameless, You call me to be perfect like You are." Praise the Lord, one day His purpose in choosing us shall be realized. No matter how weak and useless and blameworthy we currently are, one day we shall be brought by God to the place where we can stand before Him holy and without blemish as He is. This is what God has chosen us for and called us to. Since He has so desired, it shall certainly be done. And thus we know before Him what a blessed hope we have, which hope is to be like God.

Next we must consider the matter of God's inheritance in the saints. Again, let us read the pertinent part of Paul's prayer: ". . . having the eyes of your heart enlightened, that ye may know . . . what [are] the riches of the glory of his inheritance in the saints" (1.18). What is God's inheritance in the saints? The meaning here is not that of God giving inheritance to the saints, but the saints themselves being God's inheritance. Paul declares that the inheritance which God receives in the saints is glorious, even the riches of glory!

In both Ephesians 1.5 and 1.11 the word "foreordained" is used. In verse 5 we read: "Having foreordained us unto adoption as sons through Jesus Christ unto himself, according to the good pleasure of his will"—This shows us that we are foreordained to sonship. And verse 11 states this: "In whom also we were made a heritage, having been foreordained according to the purpose of him who worketh all things after the counsel of his will"—This indicates that we are foreordained to become His inheritance. So that what is said in verse 5 and what is mentioned in verse 11, though different, are nonetheless joined together.

From eternity to eternity God has a plan; that is to say, He wants sons. Many Christians cannot envisage the greatness of this matter of sons. Yet we know from Scripture that God's purpose is to obtain sons

and that His plan is related to sons. Two passages will
suffice to show this: (1) "Because ye are sons, God
sent forth the Spirit of his Son into our hearts, crying,
Abba, Father" (Gal. 4.6). This verse tells us how God
places the Spirit of His Son in us that we may be sons.
And (2) "It became him, for whom are all things, and
through whom are all things, in bringing many sons
unto glory . . ." (Heb. 2.10) This fragment of Scripture discloses that at the time when God's purpose is
realized there shall be many sons in glory, for the beloved Son of God will bring many sons into glory.
God's purpose is to obtain sons, and these sons, in
turn, are His inheritance. For this reason, God reveals
to us in Ephesians chapter 1 that He has foreordained
that on the one hand He shall obtain sons (v.5) and
on the other hand He shall gain an inheritance in
them (v.11).

What is meant by the inheritance of God? God's
inheritance means that something belongs to Him.
God has foreordained us saints to be His inherited
possession as well as His sons. All the saints belong to
Him. Paul expects us to have our eyes enlightened to
see the riches of the glory of God's inheritance in the
saints. What is this glory? Quite simply, to be like
God, to be able to glorify Him. And this is what He
wants. Hence God has chosen us to be His—to be His
sons and to be His inheritance. May the Lord open
our eyes that we may perceive how glorious this is!

God wants us to understand that not only He himself is what we must know but His work, plan, and
purpose are also what we ought to know. Such
knowledge requires vision. Without vision all that we

see is fragmentary and temporary. For instance, with regard to spiritual service, we frequently fix our gaze on the little piece of work we have in hand. We are elated when our little work seems to go well; we feel dejected, though, when our work does not go smoothly. Our view is often circumscribed within a very small scope. We fail to see greater things before God. How limited is our comprehension. It is like a little child holding in his hand a new ten-dollar bill. He feels tremendous. He looks upon this bill as his entire inheritance! Yet oftentimes our view is as small and as limited as this little child's. We do not see the whole nor the eternal. Yet we ought to know that God views *from* eternity *to* eternity. May He open our eyes lest we be small people with a small vision of spiritual things.

How small is man. We are too small, and the works of our hands are too small. God desires us to come out of this minuscule scope and to see and know experientially what is the hope of His calling and what are the riches of the glory of His inheritance in the saints. Yet this is not just something catering to men's need; it is more so something involving God's need. Why do we preach the gospel? It is not only because *men* have a need but because God too has a need. Do not infer from this that the gospel of grace and the gospel of the kingdom are therefore two gospels. Not at all, there are not two gospels; there is but the one gospel looked at from two different angles. Perceived from men's perspective it is the gospel of grace; perceived from God's perspective it is the gospel of the kingdom. Since God desires to have many people come to Him and accomplish His purpose, our work must be governed by His view as well as men's view. God wants men; He wants many to glorify Him. So that in preaching the gospel we also aim at obtaining people so as to supply God's need. God's children therefore need vision—that eternal vision. This vision will change our works, our viewpoint, and even our Christian living. Once having seen this vision we can no longer stay within the limited boundary of our small works of the past, neither can we hold on to our former views and ways. We cannot be occupied with the small gain here or the small loss there of our earlier days.

Some brothers and sisters may have heard of the eternal purpose and plan of God, but when they are engaged in preaching the gospel or in some other ministry, they may likely say: "I do not know how to join my labor with God's plan. As I am busily engaged in a work, I quickly lose sight of God's eternal purpose which I have heard. It gradually fades into the background until it is no longer seen. When I first heard about it, I was quite clear on the matter; but I later easily forgot it." Let it be emphasized right here that what we *hear* we can easily forget, but what we *see* is not so easily forgotten. It is easy to forget doctrine but hard to forget vision. Hence the question to be put is: Have you seen, have the eyes of your heart been opened by God? If you have genuinely seen His calling and His inheritance, His purpose and His plan, then whatever work you undertake—whether large or small—will most naturally be joined to His plan. When a work is not joined to His plan, it cannot be viewed as God's work.

We need to have our eyes opened by the Lord that we may have vision. This will be a great deliverance for it will free us from ourselves and from our narrow horizon. Henceforth we will deeply sense that as long as this eternal work is unfinished we can have no rest. So long as God's eternal plan is unfulfilled we will have no day of satisfaction. What our hearts are burdened with and our hands are engaged in are nothing but what God desires to have—even if what engages us is but the moving of a tiny little stone which is nevertheless built on that work which is from eternity to eternity. Let us ask God to keep us graciously in this vision. For how easy it is for us to get out from under this vision: how quickly our work may become smaller than the scope of this vision. God may not appoint us to do great things, yet He wants the works we do to be included in His wider scope. They should be joined to His great purpose and be a part of His great work. However small may be the service the Lord assigns you to do, if it is what He calls you to do, it is indeed great because it is a part of the work of God from eternity to eternity.

Know the Power of God

The Letter to the Ephesians discloses to us the mystery from eternity to eternity. On the one hand what we see is the eternity past, and in that eternity God has a foreordination, a plan, and a will. On the other hand what we see is the eternity to come, and how in that eternity God will realize His purpose and get what He is intent on obtaining. Yet between these two eternities lies the period we call time in which God discloses how He will work out the foreordained will that He had in eternity past until He obtains it in the eternity to come.

Paul in his prayer touches upon both the objective and the subjective. On the objective side the apostle prays for his readers to know God himself and to know the hope of His calling and the riches of the glory of His inheritance in the saints; on the subjective side he is intent upon their "having the eyes of [their] heart enlightened, that [they] may know . . . what [is] the exceeding greatness of his power to us-ward who believe" (1.19). After we have known God himself, together with His work from eternity to eternity, then the subjective aspect—namely, His power—begins to be exhibited in us. First the objective seeing, then the subjective working. Many Christians inadvertently change the order: they make an about-face. They set aside knowing God and His eternal purpose and deem as of first importance the inward working—that "I" can be more holy, that "I" can be more victorious, or that "I" can be more spiritual. What these believers stress is all on the side of "I" and not on the side of God. But the order which the Lord attends to is this: that because we first have known Him and His eternal will, therefore He will now work in us to reach that end. The working in us is for the sake of accomplishing the eternal purpose of God. Our personal victory and our personal work are all for that eternal purpose.

Among God's children many have upset the order. What they emphasize is their personal problem: how they can gain personal victory, personal holiness, or answers to their personal prayers. Of course, there are those who do not seek God at all, but among those saints who do seek after spirituality and do desire to go on with the Lord, many of these seem to have but one pursuit: how their personal problems can be solved before the Lord. Whatever they attend to turns out to be their personal problems. What they desire having and anticipate seeing from God are nothing but deliverances so that they may live a peaceful and happy life. Too many of His people are centered only upon themselves. Everything in their lives revolves around themselves—to such an extent that all which they are concerned with are their own selves.

Now we do indeed need the working of God in our lives, we do very much need personal victory and holiness, we are unquestionably in need of personal power and strength, and in need also of personal emancipation and deliverance. Nevertheless, the heart of the problem does not lie there. God expects us *first* to see the vision—knowing what the aim of His work is; and *then* He will work in us to arrive at His purpose. God's purpose is not merely to give us personal victory or personal holiness, for His objective cannot be so limited. He wants us to see that from eternity to eternity He has His work to do, and every redeemed person has a part in that plan of His. He works in us by the strength of His might in order that we may fulfill His eternal plan.

Therefore we must understand this very important principle: that the subjective work must be based on objective seeing, that subjective power comes from objective vision. First the vision, then the power; first the objective, then the subjective. If a person does not have vision, he cannot expect God to work in him. Suppose, for example, that a father sends his son to buy something for him. He must give his son some money. The father's motive is not that his son may have a few dollar bills in his pocket but that his son will buy things for him. So in like manner, God gives power to us not merely to give us spiritual enjoyment personally but to arrive at His goal. This matter we must resolve thoroughly before God.

Perhaps some will feel that this is too big a problem. Admittedly, it *is* big, something that is directly related to our spiritual future. Oh how many fail to receive the working of God in them subjectively because they have not obtained the vision, for all the subjective work of God is based on the vision He himself supplies. Vision comes first and then the subjective work. Initially it is objectively seeing the vision. Subsequently it is experiencing the working; first comes the knowing of God's calling and the riches of the glory of His inheritance in the saints, and then comes the knowing of the exceeding greatness of His power to usward. Consequently, we really must ask God for mercy that we may comprehend that it is not enough to be servants in His house fulfilling a little service but that we must be His friends who understand His mind. We must see, we must know, we must have vision—so much so that our hearts must be captivated by this vision. For only then will we realize that God's work is our work.

Having received the vision, however, we also must know the work of Christ in us. Unless we know the power of God in us, we are useless before Him. Vision causes us to see the plan of God while power enables us to realize that plan. Vision gives us to understand God's plan but power helps us to work out His plan. Hence the apostle shows us here that we must "know . . . the exceeding greatness of his power to us-ward who believe" as well as know the hope of His calling and the riches of the glory of His inheritance in the saints. We need not only to know God and His plan and purpose but also to know the strength of His might. We cannot say we truly know God if His power has not worked in us. We cannot say we truly know His plan and purpose if we have failed to experience His power in us. Only knowing God and His plan and purpose without at the same time knowing His exceedingly great power will merely give us something objective without having any subjective experience. We should therefore know the resurrection power of God as well as His plan and purpose.

"And [know] what [is] the exceeding greatness of his power to us-ward who believe" (v.19). This power is indeed great. It is so great that unless God opens our eyes we will not be able to see just how great it is. It is so tremendous that the saints at Ephesus did not realize the dimensions of its greatness. The immensity of God's power was beyond their comprehension. They needed Paul to pray for them that God would grant them the spirit of wisdom and revelation and enlighten the eyes of their heart so that they might apprehend its greatness. We have no way to determine how great this power is; we can only say that it *is* great—far greater than we can ever imagine.

Do not think that there is very little in the earthen vessel, which metaphor Paul uses to refer to our physical body. We learn from Paul's second letter to the Corinthian believers that there is a tremendous treasure in our earthen vessels (cf. 4.7). But do we actually believe it? In the earthen vessel is the treasure, and this treasure is precious beyond our comprehension. We need the Lord to open our eyes to see how precious this treasure is. We see on the one hand this earthen vessel—the earthly house of our tabernacle that is soon to be dissolved—and we see on the other hand the exceeding greatness of the Lord's power towards us.

God's children ought to know what they have obtained at the moment of new birth. It may have taken only a minute to have received the Lord and been born again, but it will need thirty or forty years beyond that moment to discover what each received in that one precious moment. The experience of that minute quickly becomes history, but it will take thirty or forty years' time to review it and to experience it over and over again, to have eyes opened to see how stupendous a gift God has given in that minute, and to know how exceedingly great is the power which He will manifest in their lives thereafter. Regeneration seems to be such an ordinary thing, yet to the people whose eyes are opened the power which God has demonstrated in their lives is beyond measure. Regeneration may occur within a very short time frame, but those with perceptive eyes will declare that this is a life of eternity, that this life shall live forever—that this power, in short, is exceedingly great. No child of God can fully know on earth the extent of what God has given him at the moment of regeneration. Nevertheless, blessed are those who know somewhat more.

Our spiritual progress is not judged by how much power we obtain from the Lord but by seeing more just what kind of power this is which the Lord has given: that it is the exceeding greatness of His power. Although it is at the moment of regeneration that God puts the treasure into our earthen vessel, it takes a whole lifetime to discover how great and how precious is this treasure.

A person makes no progress if what he saw of the treasure in the day of new birth and what he now sees after ten or twenty years are exactly the same. Although ten or twenty years have indeed passed, this believer is still like a newborn baby. Yet God wants us to see through the revelation of the Holy Spirit the exceeding greatness of His power towards us. Whether we are strong or weak is really dependent upon whether we see more or less. He who sees becomes strong whereas he who sees not becomes weak.

Hence the key today is seeing. It is not because we ask God to give us something that He therefore works in us. Not at all. What He could give us has already been given and is already in us. What we must ask today is for God to grant us the spirit of wisdom and revelation that we may see, for in seeing we come into experience. When many saints in the past had to go through a spiritual crisis, instead of God granting them an additional supply of strength they leaped with joy, exclaiming: "Thank God, this I already have!" Back then they were not pleading and pleading for that which they did not have; rather, those saints came to see that they had already possessed what they looked for. And thus they could raise their voices in praise and thanksgiving. No one who has not seen can begin to imagine how great is this power of which Paul speaks.

Just how exceedingly great, then, *is* this power? "According to that working of the strength of his might which he wrought in Christ" (vv.19b-20a). Let us pay special attention to the word "according." We must understand that the power which God shows to those who believe is according to the working of the strength of His might in Christ. In other words, to the extent that the exceeding greatness of the power of God worked in Christ to that extent shall the exceeding greatness of the power of God work in the church. Whatever the degree of power God worked in Christ, He will to the same degree work in us who believe. Both shall be the same! Have you seen this? If you have not, you must pray. Do not assume that because you have read the Letter to the Ephesians several times and are now able to recite by memory chapter 1 verses 19 and 20 that you have got it. Memorizing does not count here; only revelation does.

Paul *prayed* in his day for the saints in Ephesus

that they might see the exceeding greatness of the power which God had already given them. Now if we today do not see that the power in us and the power in Christ is one and the same power, we too must *pray* for seeing. If the power manifested in us is less than the power that was manifested in Christ, we should acknowledge that there are still many things which we have not seen. Let us humbly confess and pray to God to make us see. Yet whether we see or not, the fact remains that the power which God works in those who believe is according to the working of the strength of His might which He wrought in Christ. Hallelujah! This is the spiritual fact. Let us ask God to open our eyes that we may truly perceive and understand. We will not ask Him to pour upon us more power from outside; no, we will only ask Him to cause us to discover and to see more that is in us already. And when God opens our eyes to see, we shall praise Him more and more for what we have been given.

Let us now look at what this power has done for us. "According to that working of the strength of his might which he wrought in Christ, when he raised him from the dead" (vv.19b-20a). This power caused Christ to be raised from the dead. Oh! Every time we muse upon resurrection we feel its preciousness. Resurrection is that which death has no power to hold (see Acts 2.24). Death cannot contain it.

Never has any man entered into death and come back to life again. People have died throughout all the ages and the generations of mankind. And all who have entered into death have been held by death and have not returned. But there is one man who came out of death. And this man is the Lord Jesus Christ. "I am the resurrection," Jesus said, "and the life" (John 11.25). He is life, therefore all who believe in Him shall never die; He is resurrection, therefore all who believe in Him, though they die, shall live. In retrospect, all who have ever entered into death have been held by death; none has ever come out. But there is a power which can enter into death and come out of it. And this power is the power of God. Now when you observe a person dying whom you would like to see continue living, you begin to understand how great is the power of death. It is quite easy for people to enter into death, but it is impossible for them to come out of it. People may reject life but they cannot reject death.

Satan on the one hand works through darkness and on the other hand through death. Yet there is a power which comes from God: It is able to pass through death and not be held by death. The power of the devil cannot overcome it, neither can the power of Hades swallow it. It is called resurrection. That which can pass through death and not be affected by it is called resurrection. And the power that is now in us is this very power! This power which has raised Christ from the dead will also cause us to pass through death and not be held by it. For as this power once raised the Lord Jesus from the dead, so it shall also raise us from the dead.

Now this power of God not only caused Christ to be raised from the dead, it even also "made him to sit on [God's] right hand in the heavenly places, far above all . . .: and [God] put all things in subjection under his feet, and gave him to be head over all things to the church'' (vv.20b-22). Here we learn that God has made Christ head over all things, and this is for the church. Christ is made head over all things that the church may be benefited. Consequently, the church may receive from the Lord the supply of this power. Now since the power in us is such a power, and we have such a treasure in us, what else can God give us if we still fail as Christians? We should say to Him: "Do not give any more, for You have done it all." Let us see that this power is today within us, and there is therefore no problem we Christians cannot solve and no temptation we cannot overcome. For the power in us Christians is the resurrection, that power which surpasses anything else and which put all things in subjection under the feet of Christ. It works according to the working of the strength of God's might which He has wrought in Christ.

In writing the Letter to the Ephesians, Paul is exceedingly careful. He suspects that we may misunderstand such subjective work as being purely a personal matter; so that he immediately adds this fragment to his words: " . . . the church which is his body, the fulness of him that filleth all in all" (v.23). This subjective working is not for personal reasons alone, it is much more so for the sake of the body. Furthermore, this indicates that God wants us to know how His eternal plan is related to the church and not just to individuals. What is associated with the eternal purpose of God is the church: it is the church in eternity past, in the eternity to come, and in the work of God today. It is preeminently the church, not the individual.

Please understand that when power is manifested in you today it is for the church and not primarily for your personal self. God wants the church and not just the individual to have this power. Do realize that you cannot obtain the power all by yourself. And for this reason, then, we should look to God for grace that we may see what the body of Christ is. Our lives need the protection of the entire body; individual members are useless. The preservation of life is in my life not being destroyed as well as others' lives not being destroyed. If, negatively speaking, one blood vessel is broken and bleeds unceasingly, the whole body will eventually die. On the positive side, though, if the ear hears, the whole body hears; if the eye sees, the whole body sees. What one member receives, all the other members share in. Thus we must learn to live in the body: let us learn not to think of ourselves more highly than we ought to think, let us learn to treasure the church, and let us learn to walk with all the children of God. And in so doing, we shall see that the body is the vessel for the preservation of life. Said Paul, "The church . . . is his body, the fulness of him that filleth all in all." This exceedingly great power is what those who know the church have experienced. Whoever does not see the church nor deny himself will not be able to experience this great power. For this reason, when we talk about the subjective work of God in us, we must take the *church* as the unit, not the *individual*.

May the Lord open our eyes that we may truly see what God is doing in us. The exceedingly great power does not come to us as additional grace; rather, it is experienced through seeing. So that the basic question is revelation. It is in seeing; mere hearing is useless. You have heard a great deal of teaching, but if you have no revelation you will not witness His power in your life. What you have heard is like a dead account which can never be collected. May God deliver us from such dead accounting as so often teaching can become. We should ask Him to give us the spirit of wisdom and revelation that we might truly see.

Need Revelation

We have already explained somewhat concerning Paul's prayer for the saints found in Ephesians 1. This prayer's main point is that God's people may receive from Him the spirit of wisdom and revelation and thus have their eyes opened to see several things. What Ephesians 1 especially discloses to us is the fact that all the works of God have been done and that what we need today is not that He may perform again but that He may give revelation on what He has already performed. God already has His plan and will; today His children need to know what His plan and will are. "He that cometh to God must believe that he is" (Heb. 11.6). We must see that, because God "is," He therefore never changes. So that the prayer of the apostle in Ephesians 1 is that the Lord may give us the spirit of wisdom and revelation that we may truly know this God who already "is," to know in truth the work He has already done as well as the plan He has already designed.

Many people conceive before God this thought,

that it will be best if in God's plan there can be new divine determination and new divine work. The apostle, however, shows us that this is not so—that it is not a question of how best it would be if His plan were executed in this or that way, because God has already decided and we are simply to discover what He has decided. We need the spirit of wisdom to comprehend the work He does and we need the spirit of revelation to know the work He has already done. And as soon as we see this we shall have new experience and shall be useful people in His hand.

Paul reveals to us here that God's work has two parts: the one part He undertook before the foundation of the world, the other He executed on the cross. All which pertains to His eternal plan was done before the foundation of the world, whereas all which is related to man's fall and defeat was dealt with on the cross. In eternity God already has a call, an election, and a predestination. Whatever He intends to do has already been decided before the foundation of the world. There He has chosen and preordained, and nothing can shake it. In fact, after the creation of the world, man fell and Satan came in to destroy God's work; yet thank the Lord, how exceedingly great is the power which He manifests towards those who believe: there is indeed the fall, but there is also redemption: there is indeed death, yet there is also resurrection. God has an eternal plan and He has a redemption through the cross. His eternal plan seems to have been thwarted by the fall of man; nevertheless, what the fall may thwart, resurrection can rescue and restore. The cross is able to deal with the fall, and resurrection is able to get rid of death. We notice that the work of God is accomplished through the cross and resurrection.

Sometimes men are tempted to say: "If only before the foundation of the world God had made such and such a decision, how good it would be." But Paul tells us that what God has predetermined before the foundation of the world is perfect and complete. Men may even be tempted to say: "Ah, if only today God would do such and such." Yet God wants us to understand that everything has already been done on the cross and in resurrection.

Hence, Paul is not found praying that God may do a little more for us, neither that He will make His grace towards us a little richer, nor that He will manifest His power in us a little more. No, Paul's prayer is that God will give the spirit of wisdom and revelation in the full knowledge of Him, having the eyes of our heart enlightened that we may see and know what is the hope of His calling, what are the riches of the glory of His inheritance in the saints, and what is the exceeding greatness of His power towards us who believe. What Paul longs for us is not that we may obtain more of God but that we may see how glorious and rich and great is that which we have already obtained. So that what is to be received in consequence of Paul's prayer in Ephesians 1 is vision.

How many Christians there are who are still expecting something, as though God had never worked in their lives nor given anything to them. Yet what is very special about Ephesians 1 is Paul's desire to show the believers that God has done everything and accordingly there is nothing left for Him to do. He has done it in eternity and He has done it on the cross and in resurrection; with the result that today there is but one matter in question, which is, whether we see or do not see. Today's problem is not "Will God work?" but "Do we see what God has already worked?" The difference between them is vast.

Suppose a certain brother has a very bad temper (for the time being we shall use this poor illustration as an example). He tries once to overcome it but he cannot. He tries the second time to deal with it but he fails. For the third time he tries to resist it but again he is not successful. Whereupon he thinks in his heart: Why does God not do something about my temper? He seems to blame the Lord for not doing something. We see here that this brother's trouble lies in his expecting God to do a work on behalf of his temper. He reflects that if God will but move His hand everything will be fine. Yet Ephesians 1 says that God "hath blessed us with every spiritual blessing in the heavenly places in Christ" (v.3). "Hath" means it has already been done. God's thought is not in our asking Him to do more; instead, He wants to open our eyes that we may see what He has already done. Yet we tend to pray: "O God, why do You not give me greater power so as to drive away my bad temper and many other unpleasant things?" We ask for greater power, yet the Bible tells us we do not need greater power but the spirit of wisdom and revelation that we might realize the exceeding greatness of the power already in us. If one day the Lord opens our eyes to see the greatness of the power in us, then we shall shout triumphantly that there is nothing greater than this!

Do we realize that resurrection power is God's greatest power? In the Bible God has displayed for us this one fact, that the resurrection stands as the consummation of His work. In the resurrection God has done His greatest work, and He therefore wants our eyes to be opened that we may see that He can do no more than resurrection. For what He has done in Christ is the peak of His work, and there is nothing left to be done. Let us truly praise our God that His work is already completed and that nothing can be added to it. May the Lord open our eyes today that we may see this; for once we see the exceeding greatness of this power, we shall immediately experience it in our lives.

How unfortunate among the children of God that the deliverance many of them expect is a future deliverance: it may happen tomorrow or perhaps next year. Yet what God greatly wants His children to see is a deliverance already accomplished—one which needs no waiting for fulfillment. In the minds of many saints their victory is a thing of tomorrow. The answer to their hope, expectation or prayer lies in the future. But if we have revelation we shall see God's accomplished fact. Revelation unveils to us what the Lord has already done, not what He is going to do. Yet many expect to be delivered in some future day from the weakness or failure they have in their lives. If only they would let God open their eyes, they would understand that this weakness or failure has already been dealt with on the cross. And then they would praise God, saying: "O God, I thank You and praise You, because You have already done it. Thank You and praise You, this is already fully overcome."

For those of us who have experienced this, we often sense the preciousness of Ephesians 1, because it shows us that our forgiveness of sin, our redemption, and the receiving of the Holy Spirit are all accomplished facts. This passage firmly suggests to us that we already have all things and that there is but one thing we lack, which is revelation. If this missing element is present, everything will be fine. Why is it we still have such weakness? Because we do not see. Why is it we are still so useless? Because we do not see. Why is it that when the Lord Jesus was on earth He had such power and yet we are continually powerless? Again, because we do not see. The power which God shows to those who believe is according to that working of the strength of His might which He worked in Christ. It is *this* power which God gives to us. The only problem lies in the fact that we today do not see as our Lord sees. The distinction is not in the kind of power or degree of power but in seeing or not seeing. What we lack today is revelation. All will be well if we have that.

This is why we must emphasize the need for revelation. Merely listening to messages on the subject is useless; the element of seeing must be there. Revelation, not just doctrine. We may study the first chapter of Ephesians till we can memorize it, but we will not experience the power of which it speaks. Not until one day we see will we really be transformed.

Paul prayed "that the God of our Lord Jesus Christ . . . may give unto you a spirit of wisdom and revelation." Without the Holy Spirit, what profit is there in clearness of teaching? It is the Holy Spirit who opens our eyes and causes us to see. When He truly opens our eyes we will immediately be able to say: "Thank God, the work is done." We are not to expect the Lord to give us greater power: we are simply to perceive how great is the power which He has already given us. The spirit of wisdom will make us understand and the spirit of revelation will make us see; wisdom will make things clear and revelation will bring them to us.

Perhaps we have heard many times concerning the eternal purpose of God and the place of the church in His eternal plan. Yet when do we begin to be identified with God's eternal plan? It begins with revelation, because this shows us what He has accomplished on the cross as well as what He has preordained in eternity past. It is this revelation which causes us to see the eternal predetermination and work of the cross. It is also the same revelation which makes us see and know the power of God manifested in our lives. This very unveiling causes us to be a part of the church and makes us useful vessels in God's hands.

These words may be quite familiar with some people, nonetheless we must once again realize before the Lord the importance of revelation. We believe God in heaven is concerned today about His revelation because He has already done what He had intended to do. We therefore need not ask for anything except to pray for our brothers and sisters to see just as Paul prayed for the brethren of his day. Oh that God would give us all the spirit of wisdom and revelation. Let us pray humbly before Him: "O God, I want to see, I want to see!"

2 | Christ: the Rock of the Church

Now when Jesus came into the parts of Caesarea Philippi, he asked his disciples, saying, Who do men say that the Son of man is? And they said, Some say John the Baptist; some, Elijah; and others, Jeremiah, or one of the prophets. He saith unto them, But who say ye that I am? And Simon Peter answered and said, Thou art the Christ, the Son of the living God. And Jesus answered and said unto him, Blessed art thou, Simon Bar-Jonah; for flesh and blood hath not revealed it unto thee, but my Father who is in heaven. And I also say unto thee, that thou art Peter, and upon this rock I will build my church; and the gates of Hades shall not prevail against it. I will give unto thee the keys of the kingdom of heaven: and whatsoever thou shalt bind on earth shall be bound in heaven; and whatsoever thou shalt loose on earth shall be loosed in heaven. (Matt. 16.13–19)

"Who Say Ye That I Am?"

"Who do men say that the Son of man is?" This was the question that the Lord Jesus asked His disciples. There was no doubt that He was the Son of man. Everybody—both the Jews and the Gentiles—recognized and acknowledged Him as such. The question now raised was not whether the Lord Jesus was the Son of man but who this Son of man was. The Lord was not eager to know what men were speaking of Him—whether good or bad; He simply wanted to know who men were saying that He was. What, then, *did* men say about Him? Those who opposed Him said that He was demon-possessed or that He was a gluttonous man and a winebiber. We will not dwell at all on these blasphemous words. But among those who had good feelings towards Him, different views were held. Some said He was John the Baptist; some, that He was Elijah; and some, Jeremiah or one of the prophets. Nicodemus said He was a teacher who came from God (John 3.2); the Samaritan woman at the well said He was a prophet (John 4.19). Who was this Son of man? Different people held different views.

But the question posed by the Lord Jesus did not stop at this point. What He really wished to know was this: How different was the view of the disciples from that of other men? He especially desired to know what difference the knowledge of Peter towards Him was from that of other men. What He attempted to focus upon was this: People say I am this type of man, but what do you say of Me? You who are called My disciples, who do you say that I am? This was the real question He had in mind.

Simon Peter answered Jesus' question. He told the Lord: "Thou art the Christ, the Son of the living God." His answer was most clear. In it He confessed two things about the Lord: first, he confessed Jesus as Christ, and second, that He is the Son of God. As to the person of the Lord Jesus, He is the Son of God; as to His work, He is God's Christ. The Son refers to who He is; the Christ refers to what He does. "Son" indicates His relationship with God himself; "Christ" speaks of His relationship to God's plan. In speaking of the Lord himself, He is mentioned as being the Son of the living God; in speaking of the Lord's work, He is said to be Christ—He is the Christ of the living God, the Anointed One who is especially appointed to fulfill God's plan. This then, is Peter's confession—which also is our confession of the Lord Jesus.

After Peter's confession, the Lord Jesus spoke to him, saying, "Blessed art thou, Simon Bar-Jonah; for flesh and blood hath not revealed it unto thee, but my Father who is in heaven." Such confession neither originated in Peter's mind nor was learned by him from other people but was revealed by the Father who is in the heavens.

The Lord continued further by declaring: "And I also say unto thee . . ." He first showed Peter where this confession came from, and then caused His disciple to see the greatness of the effect of such confession. What did the Lord tell His disciple? "Thou art Peter, and upon this rock I will build my church; and the gates of Hades shall not prevail against it." This declaration by our Lord tells us what the foundation

of the church is. How exceedingly vital is this matter
to Christianity. It is the very core of all questions.
What, then, is the foundation of the church? The
Lord suggests to us here that the church is built on
what He terms "this rock." Hence the foundation of
the church is "this rock" of which the Lord speaks.

What This Rock Indicates

Now just what does the term "this rock" indicate?
For unless we know what this phrase means, we will
not be able to understand what the foundation of the
church is nor see clearly how the church is built up.

The rock is none other than the confession which
Peter makes concerning the Lord; and what he con-
fesses the Lord to be is the Christ, the Son of the living God. And the church is built on this very confession. She is built on men's confession and knowledge
of the Lord Jesus.

This confession of Peter is not shown him by flesh
and blood, rather it comes from the revelation of
God. So that what Peter receives is not in the mode of
traditional Christianity. It is not because people tell
him that Jesus is the Christ that he says Jesus is the
Christ. Neither is it because people tell him Jesus is
the Son of the living God that he then says Jesus is the
Son of the living God. Nor does Peter spend time in
research and thought until he himself comes to the
conclusion that Jesus is the Christ, the Son of the living God. This knowledge does not issue from Peter's
own thought nor is it suggested to him by other people, but it comes directly through the revelation of the

Father who is in heaven. This confession is not based on personal opinion nor on people's teaching but on God's revelation of His Son to Peter's own spirit. Only in this manner does he know that Jesus is God's Christ and God's Son.

Now the church is built on this confession—a confession grounded in God's revelation that shows to men the person and work of Christ. When the Father who is in the heavens reveals His Son to Peter, He causes Peter to see how Jesus is indeed God's Son and is also God's Christ. So that when the Lord subsequently declares to His disciples that "upon this rock I will build my church," this rock has direct reference to what Peter has just confessed—namely, "Thou art the Christ, the Son of the living God." This is God's revelation as well as man's confession. In short, "this rock" is none other than Christ himself.

The Rock is Christ, the Son of the living God. As regards the Lord's person, He is the Son of God. This knowledge is absolutely necessary to men. In knowing the Lord it is not so much a matter of what we know about His deeds as recounted in the Gospel records as it is of knowing Him as the Son of God. That which men see and hear and touch is not enough, for He is far greater than that: He is none other than the Son of the living God. How much easier it is to recognize Him as the Son of man—both His friends and foes confessed Him and still confess Him as such. But those who have received revelation from God, they alone know Him as the Son of God.

Whether a person has life before God or not depends on whether or not he knows that Jesus of Nazareth is the Son of God. Observe what other Scriptures say: "This is life eternal, that they should know thee the only true God, and him whom thou didst send, even Jesus Christ" (John 17.3). "That ye may believe that Jesus is the Christ, the Son of God; and that believing ye may have life in his name" (John 20.31). "He that hath the Son hath the life; he that hath not the Son of God hath not the life" (1 John 5.12). To know Jesus Christ as sent by God is eternal life. To recognize Him as the Son of God is also eternal life.

The Bible tells us that the Son of God is "the effulgence of [God's] glory, and the very image of his substance" (Heb. 1.3); He is "the image of the invisible God" (Col. 1.15). The Son of God is God himself manifested among men. For "no man hath seen God at any time; the only begotten Son, who is in the bosom of the Father, he hath declared him" (John 1.18). Therefore, if anyone wants to know God he must know the Son of God, because he can know God only through His Son. All the fulness of the Godhead dwells in Him bodily (Col. 2.9), for God manifests himself through His Son. The very essence of the Son of God is God himself, and the very expression of the image of God is His Son. "He that hath seen me," declared Jesus, "hath seen the Father" (John 14.9). And on another occasion He said this: "I and the Father are one" (John 10.30). God who dwells in light unapproachable is the Father; God who is manifested to be seen and touched by men is the Son: "The Word became flesh, and dwelt among us (and we beheld his glory, glory as of the only begotten from the Father), full of grace and truth"

(John 1.14). The Lord Jesus is the Word become flesh, and this Word in the beginning was with God, and this Word was God (John 1.1-2). "Word" is a person's expression, hence "word" represents the person. When an individual speaks, it causes people to know what kind of person he is. The Son of God is thus the uttered word of God: through Jesus as the Son men are able to understand and know God. The Lord Jesus is the Son of God, the very expression of God. He is God "manifested in the flesh" (1 Tim. 3.16). In short, He is God.

To know the Lord Jesus as the Son of God is to know Him as having the life and nature of God, to know Him as the manifestation of God, and as God himself. For in reality a person who does not know the Lord Jesus as the Son of God does not know God: "Whosoever denieth the Son, the same hath not the Father: he that confesseth the Son hath the Father also" (1 John 2.23). God has raised the Lord Jesus from among the dead to declare Him as the Son of God with power (Rom. 1.4), because it is God's will for men to know the Lord Jesus as His Son and then to know Him through His Son.

What causes us to confess that the Lord Jesus is the Son of God? It is the revelation of God in us that enables us to have such knowledge. It is the Father who is in the heavens who tells us that the Lord Jesus is the Son of God. Even though Jesus performed many miracles while on earth—all of which proved that He is the Son of God—yet men did not confess Him as the Son of God because they saw these miracles performed by Him (in fact, many people who personally saw the Lord performing these miracles would not confess Him as the Son of God). And today people believe that the Lord Jesus is the Son of God without even having seen any miracle. Peter did not acknowledge the Lord Jesus as the Son of God because he came to know Him so well through years of following Him. No, no. There is none who possesses such ability. Only one reason can explain how a person could know the Lord Jesus: the Father gives the person revelation from above: he can confess the Lord Jesus to be the Son of God whether he has seen any miracle or not because the Father in heaven has given him revelation.

What is the church? It is a group of people whose eyes have been opened by God to know that Jesus of Nazareth is the Son of God. Such inward knowledge as this can withstand any trial. What those in the church have known inwardly cannot be shaken. They may forget what they have seen or heard outwardly, but they can never forget what they have inwardly received. Hallelujah, they truly know the Lord Jesus!

God not only causes us to know the person of the Lord Jesus, He also gives us to see the ministry of the Lord Jesus. As has been mentioned, the person of the Lord Jesus flows out of His being the Son of God whereas the ministry of the Lord Jesus flows out of His being the Christ of God. The Greek word "Christ" is "Messiah" in Hebrew, and means "the anointed"—which term is related to the work of God. We observe in the Old Testament period that when people were set up by God to be priests, prophets, or kings, they would be anointed with oil. And hence the term "the anointed" carries within it the idea of receiving God's trust, accepting His commission, doing His work, and fulfilling His plan.

Now the Lord Jesus is *the* Anointed of God, which means that the eternal plan of God is to be accomplished through Him. In the eternity without beginning, the Lord Jesus is the Son of God. At the commencement of the execution of God's eternal plan the Son of God becomes the Christ of God who is destined to accomplish this eternal plan of God. The Christ of God is also eternal in character, but Christ begins with the eternity with beginning while as the Son of God He exists in the eternity without beginning. The Son of God has no beginning just as God has no beginning, but the Christ of God begins with the carrying out of God's eternal plan, since Christ is set up for the accomplishment of that plan. The Anointed One is set apart to work specifically for God. From that time onward the Son of God has become God's worker, messenger, and Christ. All the works of God—together with all His expectations and aims—are now upon His Son. So that the Son of God is now not only God's Son but also God's Christ.

For a Christian to be useful to God he must see His eternal plan. It simply is not enough for him to know that he has sinned, that the Lord Jesus has accomplished redemption for him, and that in accepting Him he shall be saved. Such a Christian will not perish, but he is of little use in God's hand. God does not establish the church merely to obtain this kind of person with which to populate it. No, He sets up the church in order to secure a people who know what is

His will and plan in Christ. This knowledge requires revelation of the Father who is in the heavens. And thus shall we see that the Lord Jesus is God's Christ—that He is the Anointed One—and the Head of the church which is His body that partakes of His anointing. How we who are His children need to confess the Lord Jesus as Christ, and to confess ourselves as Christians. We belong to Christ, and we also partake of the anointing.

One day when God opens our eyes to see, we shall begin to realize after having been Christians for so many years how small is our horizon and after so many years of work how restricted is our scope of activity. There must come such a day when God puts us in His anointing and we come to see how great a work He has done. The surprising thing is, however, that some people profess to have received the outpouring of the Holy Spirit and yet they have not entered into the work of God nor have seen the purpose of His giving them this anointing. We must ask God to open our eyes that we may know for what purpose the Lord Jesus has been anointed and for what purpose the church has been anointed, because the oil which the church receives is the same oil with which the Head is anointed. The church receives her anointing under the Head.

We need to know the Lord Jesus as the Anointed of God as well as the Son of God. We must see Him as the Anointed who fulfills the eternal purpose of God as well as the One who has the life and nature of God. Through this Son of God we know God himself, while through God's Christ we know God's plan.

If we know the Lord Jesus as the Son of God but do not know Him as the Christ of God, we will still be unable to understand what God creates us for, what He saves us for, and what He will obtain in the church. Hence we should have these two sides of knowledge concerning "this Rock"—our Lord Jesus.

This Rock is what the Father reveals to Peter. How we need God to show us what a great Man the Lord Jesus is. We must see this inwardly, since this is not anything the flesh and blood can show. Blood is related to the soul and flesh is related to the body. Neither the soul nor the body can help us know this Man whom God has set up. At first many people saw this Man on earth, but few knew Him. Many had also thronged Him, nonetheless only a few touched Him. Many were healed by Him but still only a few knew Him. How totally useless is man's thought and man's feeling in this regard.

Once the Lord Jesus said to His disciples: "Blessed are your eyes, for they see; and your ears, for they hear. For verily I say unto you, that many prophets and righteous men desired to see the things which ye see, and saw them not; and to hear the things which ye hear, and heard them not" (Matt. 13.16–17). The Lord's disciples were indeed blessed, yet this was still not sufficient for them to be in the church as members of the body, because Peter had already received the blessing which the Lord Jesus spoke of here. Had not Peter already seen what the prophets and the righteous men wished to hear? Even so, this was not enough. Only after he had confessed the Lord as the Christ, the Son of the living God did he touch the center. His knowledge of the Lord now was very different from that in the past. Earlier he knew the Lord outwardly, but now he knew Him through the revelation of the Father who is in the heavens. It was the heavenly Father who caused him to know that Jesus of Nazareth is the Christ, the Son of the living God. Such knowledge comes from spiritual revelation; it is inward and not outward.

No matter how many years a person may associate himself with Christians, unless he possesses this new knowledge of the Lord which Peter now had, he cannot become a part of the church. For anyone to become a part of the church he must receive revelation of the Father as Peter did. And this heavenly revelation in him causes him to know the Lord Jesus as the Son of God as well as the Christ of God. This alone makes him a part of the church.

Let us therefore remember that the church is not only built on Christ but is also built on the Christ whom God has revealed. Without revelation none can know Christ. Without revelation none can know God's Son. Such knowledge is not learned from doctrines or from books. It comes from the revelation of the Father.

Once our Lord said this to his disciples: "No one knoweth who the Son is, save the Father" (Luke 10.22). How marvelous is this statement. If we had been His disciples at that time, we probably would have asked Him, Do we not know you? Do we not know where you were born? Do we not know who your father was? Do we not know who your mother was? And your brothers and sisters, and also your cousin John? Did we not know your family affairs and even also the things about Elisabeth and Zacharias? Yet the Lord declared that no one knows who the Son is except the Father. When He said no one, He meant indeed no one. And here the Father did something special to Peter, which was to signify what He the Father knows of the Son so that Peter might know too.

There is a knowing of the Lord Jesus which comes from human instruction; such knowledge is accounted null and void by the Lord. Only the knowledge of the Father concerning the Lord Jesus is a true knowing of Him. And God alone can impart such knowledge to men. For this reason all who have not received such revelation from the Father have never known the Son. No man can come to the Father but by the Son, and no man can know the Son apart from the revelation by the Father. This revelation from heaven is absolutely necessary. And the church is built on this revelation.

The church knows this Man—Jesus—inwardly; she knows Him as the Christ, the Son of God. And this inward knowledge is the foundation of the church. For a person to talk about the church without a knowledge such as this is like cooking with a bottomless pot or drawing water with a bottomless bucket: it is totally vain and empty. Such knowledge of Christ is not learned from men, it comes from the revelation of the Father who is in heaven. "Upon this rock I will build my church," said the Lord, "and the gates of Hades shall not prevail against it." The church is therefore built on This Rock, and it is built for the purpose of stopping the floodgates of Hades.

We must understand that the Christ whom we conceive in our mind cannot stand any test, for this conceptualized Christ has neither power nor usefulness. Under *favorable* circumstances it may not be readily exposed as superficial; but whenever the gates of Hades are opened, the unreliability of such knowledge becomes immediately evident. Since it does not come from God, it cannot help in time of trial.

Peter knew the Lord Jesus, and he was severely tried. Did he ever fall? He fell indeed. But though he denied the Lord Jesus in a few minutes' time, Peter wept when the Lord looked at him and when he remembered the word which was spoken to him. Though he was defeated and was fallen, he nonetheless inwardly knew. This inward knowledge of Peter's is most precious, if we can see it: although he fell, yet because of this knowing, he immediately wept in sincere and genuine repentance: the inward knowledge of the Lord Jesus carried him through the trial.

The reason why the church is at all strong is because her knowledge of Christ comes from the revelation of the heavenly Father and not out of the conception of men. Never can Christ be truly conceived out of the cleverness of any individual, nor can Christ be made known through the eloquence of other, more gifted people. The knowledge of Christ which is produced by man's own cleverness and wisdom is not a rock that can stand firm. It easily falls down an incline when it is slightly pushed.

There is a big problem in the church today because of those whose knowledge of Christ comes only from instruction. Because others say such and such they also say such and such. This kind of knowledge is totally inadequate. This does not mean that the church does not need to preach or proclaim the gospel. It nevertheless underlines the fact that whatever is merely passed from mouth to mouth and from ear to ear is almost totally in vain. If we do not receive light from the Father who is in the heavens, if the light we have is all supplied by men, one day we will be shaken when others are shaken. That which is mere doctrine void of revelation is spiritually worthless. What is mere doctrine? That which is taught by flesh and blood—without any light from God or direct communication with Him—or that which must be memorized or comprehended with the mind is mere doctrine. Let us fully understand that it is not the *doctrine* of Christ which saves; rather, it is the Christ whom God has *revealed* that saves. Having *this* Christ we shall stand, for within us is a revelation which causes us to know the Lord in a true way, and nothing whatsoever is able to shake off this inward knowledge.

When Peter confessed, "Thou art the Christ, the Son of the living God," the Lord Jesus immediately declared: "Blessed art thou, Simon Bar-Jonah." Why? Because such a confession came not through man's instruction, but from the revelation of the heavenly Father. The Lord was not satisfied with what people said of Him; what He looked for was a confession based on revelation.

The value of such confession lies in revelation. It is quite easy today for a person to tell another that

Jesus is the Son of God. And after a while the one who has heard may answer that Jesus is indeed the Son of God. Yet such profession is not based on revelation, and hence has no value. To speak with spiritual value the church must speak out of revelation. Without it there is no true knowledge. This axiom is recognized by all who know God. If the church lacks revelation and if all she has comes from tradition, she is bound to fail. Tradition is that which is passed on from one mouth to another mouth, and on to still a third mouth. With the result being that one learns somebody's teaching from somebody else or learns about some particular doctrine at some particular place. What people then have are traditional teachings, nothing having been based on revelation. This is the failure of the church. We dare not despise preaching; quite the contrary, we emphasize it. Nonetheless, preaching or teaching cannot be a substitute for God's revelation. God desires us to receive revelation; He also wants us to speak out of revelation.

Take as an example the case of Philip the evangelist. Once he was sent by the Lord by the way to the desert to preach Jesus to the Ethiopian eunuch. When they came to a certain water spot, the eunuch asked to be baptized. "And Philip said, If thou believest with all thy heart, thou mayest. And he answered and said, I believe that Jesus Christ is the Son of God" (Acts 8.37 mg.). So Philip baptized the eunuch.

Now some people today try to imitate what Philip did then. They tell someone that Jesus is the Son of God, and after half an hour of preaching they ask the listener if he believes that Jesus is the Son of God. If the answer is positive, they then baptize him. Were they to be questioned about their procedure, they would doubtless say something like this: "Philip did the same thing, so this that we have done is quite Scriptural." This is certainly what the letter of God's word says, yet we must ask on what basis is this said. Some speaking is based on the Holy Spirit's revelation (as in the case of Philip), therefore it will reach to the innermost part of the listener's being. Someone else's speaking may *not* be based on revelation, and hence it will merely be the passing on of some words. If the speaking by the witness, preacher, or teacher is according to revelation, the Holy Spirit is likewise speaking as he is speaking. And thus what is being said will enter the listener's heart. Otherwise, people may mouth the same words that Jesus is the Son of God, yet what is said will be mere letter. Not because Philip did it once necessarily means that we can do it too with equal effectiveness. To do so would simply be outward imitation. It would not be Christianity. The foundation of Christianity rests on inward revelation and inward knowledge. That which is merely traditional or imitative is not true Christianity.

The foundation of the church lies in revelation. With revelation comes life. When we were saved, we did not substitute life with doctrine. In like manner, *after* we are saved we still must not substitute life with doctrine. If a person hears only doctrine and receives no light, what he obtains is only doctrine, not Christ. We know this will not solve his problem of life. If we wish to help a saved person, how can we just ask how many doctrines he knows and not ask whether he has received any revelation from God? Our emphasis on doctrine and not on revelation accounts very much for the weakness, failure, and barrenness of the church. How can the church *not* be weak if she is being weighed down with too many doctrines—all of which are passed from one to another without any inward revelation?

The Rock Is What Peter Confesses

The church is built on this rock which is Christ, the Son of God. This rock is the revelation which God has given to men, and this rock is the confession of man after he has received the revelation. We should see that confession itself is also very important. When our Lord Jesus was on earth He repeatedly said, "I AM" (see, e.g., John 8.24). Upon hearing this we believe, and He is then delighted to hear us say, "You Are." We know that there is one declaration God loves to hear from us, which is, that we say to Him, "You Are." And we say to the Lord, "You are Lord!" This important word, that "Jesus is Lord!", can be a most powerful declaration. Sometimes when things are in disarray and Satan mocks you by saying that you are now helpless, all you need do—even if you cannot pray at such a time—is simply to declare. You proclaim aloud: "Jesus is Lord!" And you shall instantly see that entangled things are nothing and that Satan's mocking is nothing. When you are being severely tried, you should rise up and speak this word. Whether it is in your own room or in a prayer meeting, you should say, "Jesus is Lord!"—by which you are telling Him: "You Are." The Lord loves to hear such a declaration, and we shall be strengthened inwardly as a result.

The Lord Jesus delights to hear this "You Are!"—otherwise why should He ask the disciples who He is? What use is it to ask the disciples, if they do not know? Yet why ask, if they *do* know? The Lord Jesus asked this question because He greatly desired to hear Peter spell it out. Let us keep in mind that the foundation of the church is not only set on the revelation which God gives, it is also set on the declaration of Peter after he has received the revelation. Once God has revealed His Son—His Masterpiece—to us, we speak out what God has revealed and confess the confession which He has given us. We acknowledge Jesus as the Son of God, we acknowledge Him as the Christ.

This is what the church is—the voice of Christ which He leaves on earth. God puts the church on earth to declare and to confess Christ. It would be totally unacceptable for Peter merely to say in his heart: "I believe the Lord has power and He reigns. I believe the Lord is glorious." It would not be enough only for Peter to say: "Lord, I believe You in my heart." What the Lord asks is: "Who say ye that I am?" "Ye" here points to the disciples. It is therefore expected of them to do one thing: to speak out with the mouth. What is it that is to be spoken out? "Say . . . that I am"—that is to say, to speak out the Lord himself, to say who the Lord is. Let us pay attention to this word.

We must recall again that the church is built upon

our confession of the Lord: "*Upon* this rock I will *build* my church; and the gates of Hades shall not prevail against it." If we do not see the relationship between the church and the gates of Hades, we may not realize the importance of the Lord's use of the word "say"; we may think that believing in heart is sufficient or praying alone is adequate. But if we see that the church is to stop the gates of Hades, then we shall appreciate how full of life and power and authority is this declaration of who Jesus of Nazareth is.

Many can testify of the numerous times when they encountered difficulties against which faith and prayer did not seem to produce any victorious effect until one day they rose up and declared: "Jesus, You are Lord, You are King, You have trampled the devil under Your feet, and You have destroyed all the works of the enemy!" As soon as this declaration was made, they were strangely strengthened. In this situation, the best prayer is not one of asking; the best prayer is one of declaring: "You Are!" "You Are!" is the church's declaration of faith. May we reiterate that the church is not only built on God's revelation but is also built on men's declaration of the revelation they receive. Declaration as a result of revelation is full of spiritual value. It has the spiritual power to shake Hades.

We know Peter was a talkative person whose speech was cut off by the Lord several times. Yet here the Lord not only allowed him to speak but also called him blessed after he finished speaking. For what Peter declared here represents the declaration of the church—an utterance which heaven loves to hear, yet one that is rarely voiced on earth. This is the declaration Hades fears to hear! But this also is the one which God desires after! In our prayer meetings, in worship meetings, and in our personal prayers, we should learn to say it more: "You Are." While on earth the Lord himself said "I Am"; now we take pleasure in replying with "You Are!" There is no utterance lovelier than this. This "You Are" is the foundation of the church, because her foundation is laid on the Lord himself. It is built on the confession which men make before the world and the devil concerning the Lord whom they know through revelation.

After Peter confessed, "Thou art the Christ, the Son of the living God," the Lord replied with: "Blessed art thou, Simon Bar-Jonah." Simon is Peter; "bar" means "son"; and "Bar-Jonah" of course means "the son of Jonah." The Lord mentioned his name and said, "Blessed art thou"; he even mentioned his father's name. So that the Simon who was blessed was not just any Simon but only Simon the son of Jonah. Furthermore, the Lord later on said, "Thou art Peter"—all this indicating to us that this revelation is very personal, but so also that the declaration or confession is likewise intensely personal! All who do not receive this revelation before God and do not have this confession can have no part in this blessing.

To sum up, then, we may say that this rock includes three meanings: (1) this rock is Christ, the Son of the living God; (2) this rock is Christ, the Son of the living God whom God has revealed; and (3) this rock is Christ, the Son of the living God whom Peter has confessed. "This Rock" which our Lord mentions is the sum total of all three meanings.

The Church Is Built on This Rock

"Thou art Peter, and upon this rock I will build my church." "Peter" in the Greek original (*petros*) means "a small stone" while "rock" (*petra*) connotes a massive piece of rock or stone. Our Lord's use of these two words is most meaningful. What He means to say is: "You are a small stone (*petros*), and I will build my church upon this massive stone (*petra*)." The foundation of the church is Christ himself. Christ is like a massive rock upon which the church is built. "Thou art Peter" means you, Peter, are a small stone, and you shall have a part in Christ. Here we are shown that the Lord needs many small stones to build His own church. "This Rock" is a massive stone, the foundation stone. There is only one foundation stone, but there are many small stones for the building.

The foundation of the church is Christ himself, and the church is built on Christ. This building work is still going on today. The Lord is building one small stone upon another. In view of this, anyone who desires to be a useful vessel of God in the church must know that the Lord Jesus is the Christ of God as well as the Son of God. We must see Him not only as the Savior but also as the Christ whom God has set forth to accomplish His purpose. The church must have this revelation; she must bear this testimony. She must have this declaration before she can see that the gates of Hades shall not prevail against her. All the temptations the devil can muster and all the works which death can inflict cannot stand before such a church. The church shall overcome all the power of Satan by her inward revelation and her outward word of testimony. Hallelujah! the gates of Hades shall not prevail against her and death shall be swallowed up by life; for the Lord builds His church on "This Rock!"

3 | Christic: the Great "I AM"

And Moses said unto God, Behold, when I come
unto the children of Israel, and shall say unto them, The
God of your fathers hath sent me unto you; and they
shall say to me, What is his name? what shall I say unto
them? And God said unto Moses, I AM THAT I AM.
(Ex. 3.13-14a)

Jesus therefore said, When ye have lifted up the Son
of man, then shall ye know that I am. (John 8.28a)

From eternity to eternity our God is God. Due to
the fact that He is God from eternity to eternity, He is
not limited by either time or space. Let us consider for
a few moments just how our God is not restricted by
time.

"So teach us to number our days," prayed the
psalmist, "that we may get us a heart of wisdom"
(Ps. 90.12). If men were truly wise, they would know
how to number their own days. But for the Lord, He

has no way to number days since He is God from everlasting to everlasting; as Peter observed, "One day is with the Lord as a thousand years, and a thousand years as one day" (2 Peter 3.8). To compute days in such a fashion is beyond the power of us human beings. If we were to count an hour as a week and a week as an hour we would make a mess of many things, since as human beings we cannot avoid being tied to time. God, however, looks at one day as a thousand years and a thousand years as one day! This means that He is not restricted by time, neither is He bound to time. In short, because He is God He transcends time.

In order to know God and to follow the course which is set before us, it is imperative that we see this characteristic of God as transcending time. We cannot measure the Lord by time. Whatever He does transcends it. For this reason, whenever we approach Him to obtain spiritual experience or receive spiritual help, we must learn to be delivered from the concept of time. Since God is the eternal One, we cannot circumscribe Him by such means. Hence all who seek to know Him must be freed from the bondage of the human concept of time.

God Is the "I NOW AM"

Another point of special significance is that God is the God of today, that He is the One who is always now. In other words, with God there *is* no concept of time. This does not mean, however, that the Lord has no time; it is only meant to indicate that He is not bound by it. We human beings divide time into periods. We say that one period has already passed, another period is yet to come, and still another period is what we call today or now. Whenever we humans think of time, we always think of past, present, and future. But when we come into touch with God, His "time frame" is always now—for He has no past and neither has He a future, because what has passed is still present with Him and what is yet to come is also present with Him! Again let me reiterate that we do not say God has no time: what we are trying to establish here is that time as we know it simply cannot apply to Him. Our time has tenses—both past, present, and future; but God has only the eternal now, an uninterrupted present. With Him there is neither past nor future.

In the Scriptures God has a name known as "Jehovah"—the meaning of which is that God is self-existing, that He is eternal now and forever. But in Revelation chapter 1 He is called "him who is and who was and who is to come" (v.4). This is viewing God from our human viewpoint. To us He appears to be the One who is and who was and who is to come, thus requiring there to be a past, a present, and a future with Him. Yet the Bible mentions these tenses of God only when He is viewed from the perspective of our human understanding. As for the name of God, however, He is known as the Eternal One; for with Him there is no concept of time save that of "now"—and this "now" is eternally so. For example, a father *is* born before a son. And this "is" is not only true today but also true forever. God is the God of now, He is the God of now from eternity to eternity. And this is forever true.

God himself never changes. What is considered past or future to men is totally inapplicable to Him, for He is eternally the "Now Is": He has but one period, which is "present." In the incident of Moses and the burning bush told of in Exodus 3, God revealed the name "I AM THAT I AM" to His servant (v.14). The time for this "I AM" is now. God meant to inform Moses that so far as He himself is concerned, He is the God of Now.

"Without faith it is impossible to be well-pleasing unto him; for he that cometh to God must believe that he is, and that he is a rewarder of them that seek after him" (Heb. 11.6). All who wish to be well-pleasing to God must have faith. What faith must they have? They must believe that He is. "I AM" is an acknowledgment of self-address; "He Is," on the other hand, is an acknowledgment addressed to Him by others. Men should not believe in God as the God of the future, since He has no future tense; nor should men believe in Him as the God of the past since He likewise has no past tense. How this situation will confuse the wise! For according to men's way of thinking they cannot help but divide events and circumstances into past, present, and future. But in God's mind there is neither past nor future.

Why, then, in His word is there mention made of past and future? This is because the word of God is spoken to us men. It *must* speak in such terms, otherwise our mind could not comprehend or understand.

Accordingly, when we say God is "Now Is," such a form does not signify time as we know it, rather it refers to the "NOW IS" that is resident in God himself. In His very nature there is neither past nor future, He is simply the God who NOW IS.

There is recorded in the Gospel of John chapter 8 the words of the Lord Jesus which were addressed to many children of Israel: "When ye have lifted up the Son of man, then shall ye know that I am" (v.28a). The "I AM" here has the same meaning as the "I AM" found in Exodus 3. Jesus did not say "I was" nor did He say "I am to come"; He said "I AM"— that is to say, "I NOW AM." He thus indicated that He is God, that He is the God of Now. When the Jews disputed Him on this point by saying "Thou art not yet fifty years old, and hast thou seen Abraham?", the Lord answered with these words: "Verily, verily, I say unto you, Before Abraham was born, I am" (vv.57,58). Upon hearing this statement the Jews took up stones to cast at Him. And why? Because the "I AM" which the Lord uttered here was precisely the same "I AM" He used in the preceding remark recorded in verse 28. Now the Jews fully understood the import of this "I AM"; and hence they took up stones to cast at Him. On another occasion, at the time when the Jews tried to seize the Lord, they went backward and fell to the ground when He said to them "I am" (John 18.6). For the Lord Jesus is the God "I AM"; and when such a God as this comes forth, men cannot but fall backward to the ground.

Knowing God by Transcending Time

What is the usefulness in our dwelling on this point? We need to know that this has much to do with our life. If we really see this we will be brought to a position of knowing more of God. Every one who seeks to know God must be delivered from the restriction of the human concept of time. If, as we shall soon see, one is so tightly wedded to the idea of time, he cannot even be saved! Do not think that our idea of time has little effect on our lives. Let me say quite seriously that its relationship to us can be exceedingly great. In what is to follow of our discussion we will illustrate this matter with four concrete facts. Let us take them up one by one.

Illustration 1—The Forgiveness of Sins

"And the blood of Jesus his Son cleanseth us from all sin" (1 John 1.7). When we preach the gospel we often tell people that the blood of Jesus, God's Son, cleanses us from all sin. Some of the listeners may ask, "How can the blood of the Lord Jesus cleanse all our sins?" We obligingly answer by saying that our sins are washed clean because the Lord Jesus was crucified on the cross to atone for our sins and thus His shed blood is able to cleanse us. Still these people may not understand; and they may therefore ask further: "How can this be? for Jesus Christ was crucified over 1900 years ago, and on the day He died I was not yet born and had obviously not yet committed any sins. How then can it be said that He died for one who is yet to be born and is yet to commit any sins?"

Let me ask you, How will you reply if you are confronted with such a question as this? Let me observe that as soon as you meet with this kind of question, you should know that this question can only exist because people have brought in the human concept of time. And when people bring in the matter of time, they are unable to understand the cross because the cross of the Lord transcends time.

Do keep in mind what we have already observed: that Christ is "Now Is"—that with God there is no distinction between past and future—that with Him it is forever today—that from eternity to eternity He is the same, never changing—that in having neither past nor future He is the God of "Now". So that if we introduce the factor of time, we will not be able to communicate with God. By examining the Greek New Testament we will know that the word "cleanse" in 1 John 1.7 is cast in the present tense. It does not say the blood of Jesus God's Son *cleansed* us from all sin, nor does it say the blood of Jesus God's Son *will* cleanse us from all sin. It quite clearly states that the blood of Jesus God's Son *now cleanses* us from all sin. It is not in the past nor in the future but in the present when all our sins are cleansed.

Before we Christians were saved, our minds were continually governed by the concept of time. We envisaged this Jesus to be a most distant person. In terms of space, He lived in the far away Judean country of Israel; in terms of time, He was separated from us by over 1900 years. How then could He die for us? How could a past savior save a present sinner? The Lord Jesus is a savior of past history, but I am a sinner who lives now. How could a person of the past save someone like me in the present? We were really puzzled, we could not figure this out. Not until one day when we told God: "I know nothing except that I am a sinner. I know I need to be saved. And now is the time for me to be saved." At that very instant God opened our eyes and caused us to see how Jesus of Nazareth died on the cross for us. It seemed as though Jesus stretched out His hands towards us and said, "You just come to Me. If only you do not reject Me, all will be well." There and then, with tears streaming down our faces we accepted Him as our Savior.

Tell me, now, did you at that moment think of the problem of time? And are you, even at this moment, one whit concerned with the "dilemma" of His being a historical Savior and you being a contemporary sinner? Our experience tells us that from that day of our conversion onward we never again feel uncertain about this matter of time, for we no longer consider the cross to be a thing of the past. God is the God of now. Yet how inadequate is our human language to express this! We can only affirm that God is always NOW. Even the *word* now is incapable of fully representing this characteristic of God. Oh how unsearchable is our Jehovah God!

The ashes of the red heifer mentioned in Numbers 19 is one of a number of types of the Lord's redemption. The ashes which were put in running water were in those Old Testament days sprinkled on a man's body to purify him from any defilement. The death of the Lord Jesus is like the red heifer being burnt to ashes. Historically speaking, that is to say, according to the human viewpoint, the Lord Jesus died over 1900 years ago. But one day when the Holy Spirit reveals to us the reality of what the Lord has accomplished, it is like putting ashes in running water and then being sprinkled. As soon as we receive it we are cleansed. The redemption of the Lord in the power of the Holy Spirit is not something past but is always an ever present now. The Holy Spirit is the Now of God; the Holy Spirit is the current power of God. It is the Holy Spirit who comes to open up to us the facts in God and who then quickens them into up-to-date experiences.

May we ever remember that God is the God of NOW. In Him there is no past. What we do will pass away, but what God does cannot pass away because He is the life and He lives forever. According to men, what He does may have relationship to time as something already done in the past or something yet to be done in the future. But so far as God is concerned, everything He does is ever present for He is the perfect life and He is so perfect that it allows for no growth. We, though, as human beings do have growth, and with growth there is created the past: I now grow a little bit, and after a while I grow a little bit more. And as I grow I treat the former things as that which is past. So that on the one hand there is growth, but on the other hand there is created a past history. Yet from eternity to eternity God is the same, and there can be no past in God; nothing in Him can pass away. He is the God of life and He lives forevermore. At the time a person is saved his eyes are opened to see that since the work of the Lord is not of the past but is ever present, he accepts Him as Savior. Unless we are delivered from the limitation of man's concept of time, we are unable to know the God who is not restricted by time.

Illustration 2—Co-Death with Christ

"Knowing this, that our old man was crucified with him, that the body of sin might be done away, that we should no longer be in bondage to sin" (Rom. 6.6). This passage of Paul's shows us that God has not only allowed the Lord Jesus to shed His blood for the remission of our sins but He has also put us in Christ so that when the Lord Jesus was crucified God crucified our old man with Him too. That we were crucified with Christ is a fact in God. But it is impossible for our human mind to explain this fact. Christ being crucified is clearly a matter of the past; yet how could *I* be joined to Him? How could this contemporary I have been joined to Christ who was crucified over 1900 years ago? Thank God, He opened our eyes one day and immediately we saw the light.

The Bible states that "our old man was crucified" with Christ, so we confess that we are dead. When we make such a confession we no longer think of the death of Christ as something past. We do not consider this death as merely a historical fact of 1900 years ago; instead, we take it as a fact of today. It is both living and fresh. It is in fact phrased, "was crucified"; and yet this "was" is only seen and touched now.

Let us never forget that whatever God has done in Christ is always NOW. Take the following Scripture passage as an example: "Men who concerning the truth have erred, saying that the resurrection is past already, and overthrow the faith of some" (2 Tim. 2.18). Those who err in truth do not say that there is no resurrection; they merely say that the resurrection is already past. This is what God's word calls erring in truth. We must acknowledge that the resurrection is not past, it is still here. Has the cross passed off the scene? No, it has not at all passed away. It is here even today. Has the fact of our co-death with Christ passed away? No, it is now here. For God is the God who is forever NOW. Whatever He has done in Christ is always and forever here. If we regard any point in the work of Christ as something past, that very point is dead to us. We thank God because nothing He has done in Christ is past. All is forever now. For He puts what His Son has accomplished in the Holy Spirit; and whatever is in the Holy Spirit is now and is never past.

As we view the work of the Lord Jesus *in* the Holy Spirit we find that all His works are living to us. If we look at His work *outside* the Holy Spirit, all will be mere letters, and letters are dead. If we treat these matters as simply doctrines, they are dead. Some people say that they do believe in the facts recorded in the Bible, but why are these facts not effective in their lives? Others say that they have heard the doctrine, yet they do not find the power. Still others may say that they have found in the Bible God's word, but why does it not work? All these failures are because they do not touch the fact of God *in* the Holy Spirit. For all the things in Christ, if treated as letters or doctrines, become things of the past; if they are approached in the Holy Spirit, however, they never become something past but are always present living realities.

Let us shout Hallelujah, for nothing in Christ is past but is forever now. Christ is still the great "I AM": He has not passed away and cannot pass away. Hallelujah, our Lord is never past! Everything in Him is full of life and full of the Holy Spirit. There is absolutely no way for anything in Him to pass away. If a person is truly led by God to press forward, he will realize that everything in Christ is present and not past in his life. Christ is the Lord of today; in Him there is no past. All that is in Christ is forever today. This is the experience of Christ, and this is the way we experience Christ. It is an everlasting now.

We acknowledge how inadequate is our word in explaining this matter. Only by the working of the Lord's Spirit in us are we brought into union with Christ. And being united with Him in this way, we shall see that all the facts in Christ are now and never pass away. The cross of Christ is now, the resurrection of Christ is now, the ascension of Christ is now, the coming of the Holy Spirit is now, and the filling of the Holy Spirit is now. Whatever God has given to us in Christ is now. We must not treat what He has given us in Christ as mere history—these things are forever now. Thanks be to God, up to this present hour Christ is still the One who NOW IS. He is here, He has not passed away. Praise Him, He is the God of now. He never passes away!

Illustration 3—Faith in Prayer

"All things whatsoever ye pray and ask for, believe that ye receive them, and ye shall have them" (Mark 11.24). According to human understanding, to "pray and ask for" is something done now, but the "shall have them" happens in the future. In between "pray and ask for" and "shall have them" is a gap of time. I now pray for healing of the sick, I now pray for the salvation of sinners, I now pray for the success of the work; but I do not know when the sick will be healed, when a particular sinner will be saved, and when this work will be accomplished. According to man's idea, the answer to prayer is bound to come in the future. Yet what the Lord Jesus says here is most amazing. He shows us what is *real* faith. He asserts that "all things whatsoever ye pray and ask for, believe that ye receive [Greek, *received*] them, and ye shall have them" (Mark 11.24 mg.). In our mind we often convert the word "receive" into "may receive" or "shall receive"; but such a change betrays unbelief. Only one kind of faith is real faith—which is the faith that believes that "God is." "Believe that ye received them" means for me that I believe I have now received them—that I do not wait to receive them in the future. Do we now see how this whole approach differs from our natural concept of the future, for in Christ there is no future tense. Oh, let us not take these words as just another teaching. We need to realize that this has much to do with our spiritual life. This is something about which we cannot afford to be negligent.

In the lengthy passage of Mark 11.12-24 from which the above verse has been quoted, we find that on one day when the Lord Jesus went from Bethany to Jerusalem, He felt hungry. And seeing in the distance a fig tree with leaves He went forward to see if He could find anything on it. But when He reached it He found nothing but leaves. So He said to the fig tree: "No man eat fruit from thee henceforward for ever." The Lord Jesus is thereby telling a fact. Here is a fig tree full of leaves, and yet the Lord says to it that no man shall eat fruit from it anymore forever. And He declares this with full assurance. Wherein lies the secret of such assurance? The secret is revealed in verse 24 that we quoted earlier. For what the Lord says in verse 24 follows the story of the fig tree told about in the preceding verses. Read again what verse 24 says: "Therefore I say unto you, All things whatsoever ye pray and ask for, believe that ye [received] them, and ye shall have them." Now this is exactly the way our Lord dealt with the fig tree. For He did not wait until the fig tree was dead before He declared His curse upon it. Not at all. It was when the fig tree was full of leaves that He announced that thereafter no man would eat its fruit. Though the fig tree appeared to be luxuriant at that time, the Lord Jesus nevertheless perceived with the eyes of faith that it was already dead and that no one would ever eat of its fruit again. In other words, before the fig tree had actually died our Lord had already seen the fact of its death.

Such, then, is the faith that believes "that ye received them." The fact which is seen in faith is not something realized in the future, it is something received now. Those who do not know the Lord will not know until they shall see in the future. But those who know the Lord know *now*, not in the future. They already know before they see it happen. For their knowledge is inward in character. Let us never forget that in the spiritual realm all things are now, not future. God is the "I NOW AM" and not the "I SHALL BE."

Mark 11.24 makes one other point very clear—that whatever God does is in the Holy Spirit. According to men's reasoning, past, present, and future form a logical sequence; but in spiritual things this is not so. All who have experience will agree with us in testifying that there is neither past nor future but only present in spiritual matters. People will treat many matters as being of the future, but we maintain that they *now* are. Let us thank God that in real faith things are already done.

Illustration 4—Tasting the Powers of the Age to Come

"And tasted . . . the powers of the age to come" (Heb. 6.5). How can the powers of the age to come ever be transported backwards into the present? We know that the phrase "the age to come" has reference to the millennial time. Yet the writer of Hebrews tells us that Christians today can foretaste the powers that are to be manifested in the kingdom age! How excellent are the situations of the millennium as prophesied in the Scriptures. Such, for example, as this wonderful prophetic passage: "The wolf shall dwell with the lamb, and the leopard shall lie down with the kid; and the calf and the young lion and the fatling together; and a little child shall lead them. And the cow and the bear shall feed; their young ones shall lie down together; and the lion shall eat straw like the ox. And the sucking child shall play on the hole of the asp, and the weaned child shall put his hand on the adder's den. They shall not hurt nor destroy in all my holy mountain; for the earth shall be full of the knowledge of Jehovah, as the waters cover the sea" (Is. 11.3-9). Or this that is prophesied for that time: "They shall beat their swords into plowshares, and their spears into pruning-hooks; nation shall not lift up sword against nation, neither shall they learn war any more" (Is. 2.4). How very promising is the kingdom age!

Now according to the human viewpoint, these marvelous conditions will be enjoyed some day in the future; yet Hebrews 6.5 declares that Christians may taste them today because it has been given to them by God to foretaste the powers of the age to come right now. During the kingdom age, for example, demons shall be cast out; today, though, Christians can also cast out demons. During the kingdom age, people will enjoy health; today believers too receive the quickening of the body in the Lord. In that future day all shall know the Lord; even so, today we can know Him also. In that day a weaned child can place his hand on the adder's den in safety; today those believers who are sent to preach the gospel may likewise take up serpents (see Mark 16.17-18). Hence in these and in many other ways, God's children may foretaste the powers of the age to come. Judging according to the concept of time, it would seem that these things lie yet in the future; but the church may transport them to the present.

We really ought to shout Hallelujah, for Christ "NOW IS"! Christians are in contact with this Christ who "NOW IS"—they are communicating with such a Christ as this—they are related to the God who NOW IS, so that all spiritual things are "now is" to the Christians.

How frequently you have burdens, trials, and problems. So you pray to God, yet no relief seems to come. The more you pray, the more complicated matters appear to be, as though no amount of prayers will help. You should realize that you have been standing on the wrong ground as you prayed, for you have been limiting God with time. You have been waiting for things to happen in the future, yet nothing has happened. Let us thank God that we can instead put the future and today together. Let us begin to believe that in our personal experiences we may move the conditions of the future kingdom age into the very present.

Let us ask God to cause us to see that our Lord is the God who "NOW IS"— that whoever touches this point touches the secret of communicating with Him. Let us ask the Lord to deliver us from our own thoughts, from our own cleverness, from the limitation of our earthly time concept that is bound to the past and/or the future, and from any dead knowledge which is outside the Holy Spirit. Let us ask Him to cause us to see that all things are in the Holy Spirit, that they are now and are living. May the Lord enlighten us, lead us forward, and bless us. Amen!

4 | The Vision of the Glorious Christ

I John, your brother and partaker with you in the tribulation and kingdom and patience which are in Jesus, was in the isle that is called Patmos, for the word of God and the testimony of Jesus. I was in the Spirit on the Lord's day, and I heard behind me a great voice, as of a trumpet saying, What thou seest, write in a book and send it to the seven churches: unto Ephesus, and unto Smyrna, and unto Pergamum, and unto Thyatira, and unto Sardis, and unto Philadelphia, and unto Laodicea. And I turned to see the voice that spake with me. And having turned I saw seven golden candlesticks; and in the midst of the candlesticks one like unto a son of man, clothed with a garment down to the foot, and girt about at the breasts with a golden girdle. And his head and his hair were white as white wool, white as snow; and his eyes were as a flame of fire; and his feet like unto burnished brass, as if it had been refined in a furnace; and his voice as the voice of many waters. And he had in his right hand seven stars: and out of his mouth proceeded a sharp two-edged sword: and his countenance was as the sun shineth in his strength. And when I saw him, I fell at his feet as one dead. And he laid his right hand upon me, saying, Fear not; I am the first and the last, and the Living one; and I was dead, and behold, I am alive for evermore, and I have the keys of death and of Hades. Write therefore the things which thou sawest, and the things which are, and the things which shall come to pass hereafter; the mystery of the seven stars which thou sawest in my right hand, and the seven golden candlesticks. The seven stars are the angels of the seven churches: and the seven candlesticks are seven churches. (Rev. 1.9-20)

The Book of Revelation is "the Revelation of Jesus Christ"—which is clearly stated at the very beginning of the book (1.1). "The Revelation of Jesus Christ" means that this revelation belongs to Jesus Christ. This revelation comes through Him as well as speaks of Him. God gives the revelation to Jesus Christ and through the Latter this revelation is given to us. All the revelations in the entire Bible focus on Jesus Christ and are all for the purpose of revealing Him. And hence the Book of Revelation tells us not only of future things but more so of who Jesus Christ is. Indeed, although the Bible contains many prophesies, its *central* thought and aim is not in our getting to know these prophecies, but in showing us who Jesus Christ really is. It discloses to us who is this Christ who was formerly Jesus of Nazareth on earth but who is now ascended to heaven.

In recording all the future events found in the Book of Revelation, John aims not at our knowing how and when these things will happen but at our recognizing how Jesus Christ shall reign on the throne. That Jesus Christ is King on the throne—this is what the Book of Revelation would have us to know. We know Him as the Savior, yet such a knowledge is not enough, because we must also know Him as King. We must know the severity of the Lord as well as the love of the Lord. Let us clearly understand that the purpose of Revelation is to cause us to know more of this Jesus Christ that we may be watchful and prepared till the day we shall see Him face to face.

Now our present discussion will not cover all the revelations of Jesus Christ as shown in this Book; rather, we will dwell chiefly on the very first vision God reveals to John. It is the vision of the glorious Christ.

John is called the disciple who leaned on the bosom of the Lord (see John 13.25, 21.20). But this King on the throne is what John had not learned as he rested on the Lord's bosom. Now, though, God is intent on revealing *this* Jesus Christ to him. Such a knowledge will be for John a very basic one. And once having this knowledge, it will not be hard for John to solve all the prophecies concerning coming events.

Under what kind of circumstances does John receive this revelation? "I John, your brother and partaker with you in the tribulation and kingdom and patience which are in Jesus, was in the isle that is called Patmos, for the word of God and the testimony of

Jesus" (v.9). Here we are told by John under what circumstances he receives the revelation. He does not claim that he is a great apostle chosen by the Lord. He merely says, I John am your brother and partaker in the tribulation and kingdom and patience in Jesus. He does not esteem himself higher than other people. On the contrary, he merely looks upon himself as their brother. How humble and sensitive this reveals John to be. Though his body is on the island of Patmos, his spirit is with his brethren in suffering together and patiently waiting together for the coming of the kingdom. He has such a feeling because he lives in the reality of the body of Christ.

He knows that the relationship among tribulation, the kingdom, and patience is inseparable. Before the coming of the kingdom there must be tribulation: "Through many tribulations," asserted Paul, "we must enter into the kingdom of God" (Acts 14.22). Tribulation paves the way for John to enter the kingdom, and tribulation works for him exceedingly more and more an eternal weight of glory (2 Cor. 4.17). Because John loves the kingdom he does not seek to escape from tribulation. The kingdom is definitely coming, but its coming seems so slow. Without patience, slumbering can hardly be avoided; without patience, drawing back is almost certain; and without patience, the world's attraction seems irresistible. John knows all this, and so he patiently waits. He believes that he has a part with his brothers in the tribulation and kingdom and patience that are in Jesus. Praise the Lord, John is not alone on this path.

Let me ask, are we not also brothers and sisters to

John? Yet if so, do you share with him in this tribulation and kingdom and patience in Jesus? Are you sympathetic to his feeling and his experience? Or have you chosen the broad way and travel comfortably in it? It is not because you believe in the kingdom that you enter it; nor is it because you have some knowledge of the kingdom that you therefore seize upon it. You need to realize that for you to enter the kingdom you must go the way John went; otherwise, your entering the kingdom is merely an ideal.

Due to his faithfulness in the word of God and in the testimony of Jesus, John was exiled to the island of Patmos. This island is situated in the Aegean Sea— off the Turkish coast. It is rocky and barren. From the human viewpoint, John's staying in this isolated place was too lonely and pathetic an experience; yet he neither murmured nor complained, because he knew for whom he suffered. Praise and thank God, it is in just such an environment that the glorious Christ appeared to him and gave him new revelation and a renewed trust. Oh, for John at that time the earth was receding and heaven was opening. This reminds us, does it not, of   Moses in the wilderness, David in his constant tribulation, and Paul in bonds. How these all received fresh revelations! John, then, followed in the footsteps of these men and received a vision he had never known before. He came to know the Lord who sits on the throne.

Let us now look into this vision of the glorious Christ which John saw.

"I was in the Spirit on the Lord's day, and I heard behind me a great voice, as of a trumpet saying" (v.10). "The Lord's day" here signifies the first day of the week. It is not "the day of the Lord" since the latter points especially to the day of judgment. John saw the vision on the Lord's day—the first day of the week—and not in the day of the Lord's judgment.

Now John heard in the spirit a great voice behind him. The spirit in man provides us with God-consciousness. It is that part of man for worshiping God, and it enables us to hear His voice intuitively. Here on Patmos we find the spirit of John is free and not restricted by environment. He has the ascended life (cf. Eph. 2.6). His spirit is neither subject to the siege of the soul nor affected by the latter's stimulation. He can freely commune with his Lord and receive new revelation. Though his body is confined to the island of Patmos and thus he has lost his freedom physically, nevertheless John's spirit is not imprisoned because of this. Patmos cannot block out the heaven above his head; on the contrary, the island seems to induce a contact of his spirit with heaven. How sad that God's children frequently misunderstand "the Patmos islands" of their lives that have been arranged by God!

On this Aegean island John encounters a very special experience. He is drawn by the Holy Spirit to leave behind his own personal consciousness and to enter the spiritual realm so as to hear the word of the Lord. Before God will show him the *future* glory, He draws John's attention first to the *current* conditions of the church. Hence he hears "behind [him] a great voice, as of a trumpet." He turns around "to see the voice" (v.12). And what does the voice, as of a trumpet, have to say? "What thou seest, write in a book and send it to the seven churches: unto Ephesus, and unto Smyrna, and unto Pergamum, and unto Thyatira, and unto Sardis, and unto Philadelphia, and unto Laodicea" (v.11). Here John receives a commission to write to the seven churches in Asia. Why write to only seven? Beyond just these seven churches, there were at that time others in Asia such as the church at Colosse, the church at Hierapolis (Col. 4.13), and several others. Why does God not order John to write to them as well? This is because "seven" in the Bible is a number which signifies perfection. God chooses these seven churches to represent the entire church. The various conditions of the church of God after the time of the twelve apostles and until the second coming of the Lord are represented by these seven churches.

These seven churches were in actual existence in those days. And had the Lord Jesus come to them at that time, what the seven letters said would have been fulfilled in those churches. On the other hand, the Holy Spirit is going to use these seven churches to represent all the churches after the first-century apostolic age. So that from our present perspective, the conditions of the seven churches spoken of in the seven letters can be doubly applied: first, to the actual conditions of the various churches at that period; and second, the conditions of the visible church in all ages.

"And I turned to see the voice that spoke with me. And having turned I saw seven golden candlesticks; and in the midst of the candlesticks one like unto a

son of man" (vv.12–13a). The seven golden candlesticks which John saw are the seven churches. These
serve to reflect the actual conditions of the seven local
churches then existing in the province of Asia. These
seven candlesticks are not joined in one but are individual in character, each being responsible to shine in
its respective locality. The church is one in life as one
body, but in outward appearance on earth each assembly is autonomous according to locality and each
is directly responsible to the Lord as seven individual
candlesticks. By reading Revelation chapters 2 and 3
we can see the conditions of those seven churches at
that time: their works, environments, responsibilities,
defeats, and rewards are all different. We will make a
serious mistake if we fail to recognize these
differences.

These seven churches do not bear a common de-
nomination since they are severally called the church
"in Ephesus"—"in Smyrna"—"in Pergamum"—
"in Thyatira"—"in Sardis"—"in Philadelphia"—
"in Laodicea": there is one church in each locality.
There should not be several churches in one locality
nor several localities for one church. God has ordained that in one locality there is but one church.
Hence there is only the church in Ephesus or the
church in Smyrna, never the churches in Ephesus or
the churches in Smyrna. It is also ordained by God
that a local church cannot be joined to other local
churches to form one church. Therefore the Bible
says "the seven churches that are in Asia" (Rev. 1.4)
and not "the church in Asia"—since Asia at that time

was a Roman province and in a province there were obviously a number of localities.

What God has ordained for the church is that on the inward side it must submit to the authority of the Holy Spirit while on the outward appearance side it must take locality as its boundary. If we understand the Bible and know the Holy Spirit we cannot but confess that the church on earth is to be expressed in one locality with one church. One church in several localities or seven churches in one locality is not scriptural. For to have one church in several localities demands a unity above that of Scripture; and to have several churches in one locality breaks the unity called for in the Scriptures. If we do not forget that these seven candlesticks are the seven churches, then we will also not forget the conditions which the church ought to have before God.

The Bible uses a golden candlestick to represent the church. This is very meaningful, since gold in the Bible typifies the glory of God. The responsibility of the church is to magnify the glory of God. The candlestick has no light in itself; the shining of the candlestick depends on the oil as well as the fire. If the church is to shine for Christ she must depend incessantly on the Holy Spirit of God and on the divine holy fire; otherwise, she cannot shine for a minute. How we long that the church may be "seen as lights in the world, holding forth the word of life" (Phil. 2.15–16).

"And in the midst of the candlesticks one like unto a son of man"—This speaks of Christ being with His church. The presence of the Lord is most precious, though His presence is not solely for blessing but also for inspecting. If we are faithful we should not be afraid if His presence is with us; but should we be unfaithful, how can we escape since He is in our midst inspecting us.

This one who looks "like a son of man" is none other than our Lord Jesus. Daniel too mentioned how he saw One "like unto a son of man" (Dan. 7.13). As recorded in the Gospels, our Lord often referred to himself as "the Son of man." Why is it said here that He looks "like a son of man"? To say this is in fact to suggest the *divinity* of the Lord Jesus. While He was on earth, Jesus was the Son of man; now that He has been raised from the dead, He is more than the Son of man: He is also the Son of God. Hence it says that He looks like a son of man. We know that God created man for him to rule the earth (see Gen. 1.28). Unfortunately, the first man fell and thus failed to realize this purpose. For this reason the Son of God came to this world to become a man that He might accomplish God's purpose. God clothed with the body of a man became the Son of man. This marks the beginning of the Lord as the Son of man. In other words, the Son of man is the name for God becoming man. The thirty-odd years of the Lord's life on earth is the period during which He is the Son of man. Before His incarnation He was "like unto a son of man." This is the One whom Daniel mentioned. After His resurrection, and though He still has bones and flesh (see Luke 24.39), He is more than the Son of man: He is the risen Son of God. Hence He is the Lord Jesus Christ who looks "like unto a son of man."

This Christ who is "like unto a son of man" is in the midst of the candlesticks: He is the Lord who "*walketh* in the midst of the seven golden candlesticks" (Rev. 2.1). This indicates to us that the Lord is face to face with His churches and is inspecting their conditions. He does not sit here to receive the worship of His church; He instead is *judging* His church. How we ought to fear the Lord, "for the time is come for judgment to begin at the house of God" (1 Peter 4.17).

"Clothed with a garment down to the foot, and girt about at the breasts with a golden girdle" (v.13b) —The priest of old always wore a long garment. In wearing a long garment here the Lord Jesus is shown to be a priest—nay, *the* Priest of God. As the Priest the Lord is seen walking among the churches to determine which lamp is burning rightly and which is not. Here we must recall the fact that in the tabernacle and temple of old, the light of the candlestick in the holy place could never be allowed to go out. Its light had to burn day and night unceasingly, requiring the Old Testament priest to trim the light continually and add oil to the candlestick. In like manner, then, the Lord Jesus is here seen trimming that lamp which is not burning bright; and this act of trimming is in reality a picture of judging. Christ is therefore found walking among the churches doing the work of judgment; and such judgment is according to the light of eternity.

Formerly we saw Jesus as the Lord of grace, now

we see Him as the Lord of judgment. Yet this present judgment depicted here in John's vision is the priestly judgment, pictured for us in the act of trimming. A day is coming, though, when it will be the kingly judgment when rewards will be dispensed. Every child of God must some day meet the awesome holiness of the Lord; and at that time he can make no excuse of anything. Light will eliminate all arguments and all reasonings. Light will not only enlighten, it will also kill. Light will uncover the true nature of everything and eradicate all that is incompatible with the Lord. Each time God enlightens, it slays the natural life of man. People may marshal many reasons in defense of themselves, but under the enlightening of the Lord they can find no excuse. The farther people are away from the Lord, the more self-complacent they become. Yet the light of the Lord is irresistible. How the church ought to fear the Lord, always accepting His trimming lest her light grow so dim that her candlestick must be removed and she loses her testimony.

"Girt about at the breasts with a golden girdle"—The high priest in the Old Testament period could not continue in his office because of death (see Heb. 7.23). The girdle he wore was made of gold threads (see Ex. 28. 4–5) which could not, of course, be preserved forever. But our Lord lives forever, and His priesthood is unchangeable (see Heb. 7.24). The girdle around His breasts is made of pure gold that shines forever and abides forever. Now the girdle was usually wrapped around the waist for the sake of facilitating service. At this time, however, the Lord has the girdle around His breasts. This speaks of His strength and love—the "girdle" signifying strength in movement and the "breasts" standing for love. This High Priest who walks in the midst of the golden candlesticks is full of power but also of affection. How can we not prostrate before Him with fear and trembling on the one hand and with gratitude and joyful comfort on the other!

"And his head and his hair were white as white wool, white as snow; and his eyes were as a flame of fire; and his feet like unto burnished brass, as if it had been refined in a furnace; and his voice as the voice of many waters" (vv. 14-15). All these indicate to us that not only does the Lord's *apparel* show the nature of His judgment but His very own *features* express this element as well. Let us look into these various features more closely.

"His head and his hair were white as white wool, white as snow"—Daniel the prophet saw in a vision "one that was ancient of days . . . his raiment was white as snow, and the hair of his head like pure wool" (7.9). This Ancient of Days is none other than God. Here, the Lord Jesus—whom John saw—bears the same features as did the God whom Daniel saw. This is Scriptural proof that the Lord Jesus is God. The head and hair of our Lord are white—signifying that He transcends time (and yet includes time) as well as that He is absolutely holy. When the Bible speaks of the failing and change of man it says his hairs become gray (see Hosea 7.9). In this respect, our Lord does not have a single gray hair. But on the other hand, Proverbs states that "the hoary head is a crown of glory" (16.31). Hence white hair means both experience, glory, and length of years. It also denotes holiness, for in Isaiah, God is recorded as promising to wash away men's sins that they may become as white as snow and as wool (1.18). Whenever we recall that our sins are washed as white as the head and hair of our Lord are white, we must marvel at the greatness of the Lord's grace.

"And his eyes were as a flame of fire"—A flame of fire is able to illuminate things. The eyes of the Lord are as a flame of fire, therefore He can search the reins and hearts of men (cf. Rev. 2.23). Nothing can be hidden from Him. Whenever His flaming eyes perceive something at odds with His holiness, He will judge and condemn. He is light and He himself is the Illumination. He will search out sins, causing the righteous to be preserved in purity and the evil to go to perdition.

When the Book of Malachi speaks of the Lord's appearing, it asserts that "he is like a refiner's fire" (3.2). During the time of the restoration of Israel, the Lord will purge the Jews "by the spirit of justice, and by the spirit of burning" (see Is. 4.3-4). When we stand before the judgment seat of Christ, the Lord will use fire to prove each man's work: "For the day shall declare it, because it is revealed in fire; and the fire itself shall prove each man's work of what sort it is" (1 Cor. 3.13)—"Wherefore judge nothing before the time, until the Lord come, who will both bring to light the hidden things of darkness, and make manifest the counsels of the hearts; and then shall each man have his praise from God" (1 Cor. 4.5)—"For we must all be made manifest before the judgment-seat of Christ; that each one may receive the things done in the body, according to what he hath done, whether it be good or bad'' (2 Cor. 5.10). We should remember that ''there is no creature that is not manifest in his sight: but all things are naked and laid open before the eyes of him with whom we have to do'' (Heb. 4.13). Who can escape before such eyes? Not one of us. Therefore let us sing this song today:

> Daily lift I up my eyes,
>   the light of judgment-seat survey;
> May all my life and work
>   stand the fire of that great day.*

"And his feet like unto burnished brass"—Brass in Scripture symbolizes judgment. The laver that is placed between the tent and the altar, and the fiery serpent lifted up on the pole in the wilderness are both entirely made with brass (see Ex. 30.18, Num. 21.8-9). "His feet like unto burnished brass" shows not only that His movement is full of strength but His movement, His way, and His step are absolutely righteous. His feet are like burnished brass "as if it had been refined in a furnace." When brass is refined in a furnace it gives forth a fearful color of white. How strong and pure are the Lord's feet. What His sharp eyes condemn, His strong feet trample upon! He will judge all which His eyes condemn as sinful. His actions are pure. As He walks among His churches in such fearful holiness, how many are the things which must be condemned by Him!?!

*A stanza of a hymn written by the author.—*Translator*

"And his voice as the voice of many waters"—
This voice is majestic and irresistible. It is no longer
like His former earthly voice which was so soft and
tender that it drew men to Him. Now it is so majestic
and fearsome that men are afraid to hear, and yet
they cannot fail to do so: "The floods have lifted up,
O Jehovah, the floods have lifted up their voice; the
floods lift up their waves. Above the voices of many
waters, the mighty breakers of the sea, Jehovah on
high is mighty" (Ps. 93.3-4). This shows just how
loud *is* this voice! "And, behold, the glory of the God
of Israel came from the way of the east: and his voice
was like the sound of many waters; and the earth
shined with his glory" (Ez. 43.2). This depicts the
grandeur and the power of the voice of God. And today this grandiose and powerful voice comes forth
from Christ, the One who is like the Son of man.

Concerning the power of His own voice the Lord
once said: "Verily verily, I say unto you, The hour
cometh, and now is, when the dead shall hear the
voice of the Son of God; and they that hear shall
live" (John 5.25)—just as Lazarus, whom the Lord
loved, had died and was buried in the tomb for four
days; but when the Lord cried with a loud voice,
"Lazarus, come forth," then "he that was dead came
forth" indeed! (John 11.17,43,44) How powerful is
the voice of the Lord!

Concerning His wrath we are told that "Jehovah
will roar from on high . . .; he will give a shout . . .
against all the inhabitants of earth" (Jer. 25.30). Indeed, "the voice of Jehovah is powerful; the voice of
Jehovah is full of majesty" (Ps. 29.4). When He

comes to judge, His voice alone shall make souls tremble. If the church fears the Lord and obeys His speaking in her midst, she can approach with boldness when she meets the Lord face to face.

"And he had in his right hand seven stars: and out of his mouth proceeded a sharp two-edged sword: and his countenance was as the sun shineth in his strength" (v.16). Concerning the One who is like the Son of man, we have already contemplated a little of His holiness and majesty; now we will see something of His position.

"And he had in his right hand seven stars"— These seven stars, as we are told later, are the angels of the seven churches. That Christ is holding them in His right hand signifies His authority over them, for in the Scriptures the term "right hand" carries with it the meaning of authority and exaltation (cf. Ps. 17.7, 18.35; Acts 2.32–33). These angels (or messengers) are in the Lord's hand. They are faithful, and their ministries shine as the stars. By their being in the hand of the Lord, the position of these messengers is most secure—though their responsibility is also great. Furthermore, these messengers are in the Lord's *hand* and not located as a crown on His head, because the time of their glorification has not yet come. They should carry on their ministries faithfully so as to shine forever; otherwise, they will become like "wandering stars" (Jude 13).

"And out of his mouth proceeded a sharp two-edged sword"—Isaiah 49 states that "he hath made my mouth like a sharp sword" (v.2). This points to the power of the speech of our Lord. His words will not only smite people's consciences to convict them of sin today but will also be sharp and cutting at the time of judgment: "He that rejecteth me, and receiveth not my sayings, hath one that judgeth him: the word that I spake, the same shall judge him in the last day" (John 12.48). How we believers need to fear the Lord, because judgment shall in fact begin with the house of God!

In Revelation chapters 2 and 3 we are shown how the Lord who walks among the seven golden candlesticks uses His word to judge His churches. In commanding John to write to the angel of the church in Pergamum, the Lord said: "These things saith he that hath the sharp two-edged sword . . . Repent therefore; or else I come to thee quickly, and I will make war against them with the sword of my mouth" (Rev. 2.12,16). This sword of the mouth is none other than the word of God—for please note that "the word of God is living, and active, and sharper than any two-edged sword, and piercing even to the dividing of soul and spirit, of both joints and marrow, and quick to discern the thoughts and intents of the heart" (Heb. 4.12). And note also that "no word from God shall be void of power" (Luke 1.37). The word of God is sharp and powerful.

Accordingly, we should have the word of the Lord dwelling richly in our hearts (see Col. 3.16) so that His word might have a right place in our lives and that it may be used as a weapon against the enemy. When the Lord was tempted in the wilderness by the devil, Jesus used words from the Scriptures to overcome him. The word of God is truly sharp and powerful;

we must therefore treasure His word and trust in it.

"And his countenance was as the sun shineth in his strength"—Christ is the Sun of righteousness (see Mal. 4.2). When the Lord Jesus was on the mount of transfiguration, He for once manifested His glory. At that moment "his face did shine as the sun" (Matt. 17.2). Peter later explained that this spoke of "the power and coming of our Lord Jesus Christ" (2 Peter 1.16a; see also vv.16b-17). The sun is called "the greater light" and it is "to rule the day" (Gen. 1.16). The statement "the sun shineth in his strength" has reference to the noonday, when there is neither cloud nor mist. Hence it refers to the authority and glory of our Lord in the millennial kingdom.

When Scripture speaks of the appearing of the Lord Jesus it uses "morning star" and "the sun" as types. The appearing of the morning star is for the saints, while the appearing of the sun is for the entire world. The morning star appears just before dawn; and only the watchful may see it. In view of this, Christians should be most watchful. The sun appears in the day and is therefore seen by all people. The morning star appears first and the sun thereafter. Before our Lord appears to the world He will manifest himself first to those who have loved His appearing. What a blessed hope this is! Yet do we really love His appearing?

"And when I saw him, I fell at his feet as one dead" (v.17a). John is called the one who leaned on the Lord's bosom (see John 13.23-25, 21.20), yet here at this moment when he saw Him who is coming to execute judgment, he fell at Jesus' feet as one dead because of His holiness, glory, majesty, and power. Oh, the judgment of the Lord is serious. Who can stand such a vision!?! If this happened to the apostle John, what will occur with respect to us? May we not in the least despise the solemnity of this judgment.

If a person does not see the Lord, nothing will happen to him; but once he sees the Lord, he cannot fail to be smitten in heart and fall at His feet as one dead. While Job was arguing with his three friends, he stood up against them on the ground that he was perfect. Later, however, when he saw the Lord God, he acted differently. Said Job: "I had heard of thee by the hearing of the ear; but now mine eye seeth thee: wherefore I abhor myself, and repent in dust and ashes" (Job. 42.5-6).

When the prophet Isaiah saw the Lord sitting upon the throne, high and lifted up (6.1), he could not but cry: "Woe is me! for I am undone; because I am a man of unclean lips, and I dwell in the midst of a people of unclean lips: for mine eyes have seen the King, Jehovah of hosts" (6.5).

The prophet Daniel is one about whom the Bible never records any fault; yet upon seeing the Lord in a vision, this is what the prophet's response was: "There remained no strength in me; for my comeliness was turned in me into corruption, and I retained no strength. . . . Then was I fallen into a deep sleep on my face, with my face toward the ground" (Dan. 10.8a).

Again, what happened to the prophet Habakkuk when he heard the voice of the Lord? He confessed: "I heard, and my body trembled, my lips quivered at the voice; rottenness entereth into my bones, and I tremble in my place" (3.16).

Paul formerly persecuted and hurt the disciples of the Lord, but on the road to Damascus he fell upon the earth when a light out of heaven shone round about him (Acts 9.1–4).

If we really meet the glory, holiness, and judgment of the Lord, we cannot help but deeply abhor ourselves. How pitiful it is that so many Christians when referring to themselves—and even while confessing their sins—seem to be justifying themselves and parading themselves. And too many Christians harbor secret pride within as well as display open pride without because they have not met Christ: "The heart is deceitful above all things, and it is exceedingly corrupt: who can know it?" (Jer. 17.9) Before we see the Lord how easy it is for us to believe in ourselves, approve of ourselves, and be contented with ourselves! Only in the light of God can we see our true condition.

Hence all who are self-sufficient and self-righteous have never met the Lord nor encountered His light, for who can meet the Lord and not fall on his face? May the Lord have mercy on any person who is still exalting self and considering himself righteous. May the glory and the holiness of the Lord cause us to abhor ourselves—to fall at His feet and deliver ourselves to death so that Christ may be manifested in our lives.

"And he laid his right hand upon me, saying, Fear not" (v.17b). The Lord not only holds in His powerful right hand the seven stars but in addition lays this same right hand on John, and gently says, "Fear not." Although our Lord is in glory, He is nonetheless full of love! This tender word "Fear not" reveals the Christ of the Gospels: it unveils the loving heart of the Lord. The Book of Revelation deals basically with the judgment of the Lord, yet those who are constrained by His love and love Him have nothing of which to be afraid. For "there is no fear in love: but perfect love casteth out fear" (1 John 4.18). It is the pleasure of the Lord to reveal himself to men, but there is a class of people who feel His severity more than His loving-kindness; for them, it seems as though the more the Lord reveals himself the less they dare to approach Him. Nevertheless, we see here that the Lord laid His right hand on John and said, "Fear not." If there is nothing between us and this loving Lord He will give strength to us when we are weak and will comfort us when we are afraid.

"I am the first and the last, and the Living one; and I was dead, and behold, I am alive for evermore, and I have the keys of death and of Hades" (vv.17b–18). The mere appearing of the Lord in glory causes us to know our weakness, but even more so to know the nobleness of the Lord. The issue here is not in seeing what *we* are but in seeing what the *Lord* is. If we know what He is, we will also know ourselves.

The Lord aims at revealing himself. How comforting are these words: "I am the first and the last, and the Living one; and I was dead, and behold, I am alive for evermore, and I have the keys of death and of Hades." Because He is such a Lord, He can comfort John with "Fear not." This Lord Jesus is the first and the last and living one and who died for our sake but is now resurrected: He "was delivered up for our trespasses, and was raised for our justification" (Rom. 4.25). For this reason, in the day of judgment we can stand boldly before His judgment seat. We escape the pains of the eternal lake of fire by His death and resurrection; we also avoid the shame at the judgment seat by His death and resurrection. Let us examine ourselves to see if we really depend on the death and resurrection of the Lord. If we rely on anything else we shall surely fail.

Who are spiritually strong and ready to meet the Lord? Such do not depend on their being more excellent than other people—rather, they rely more on an experience of the Lord's death and resurrection: "For if we have become united with him in the likeness of his death, we shall also be in the likeness of his resurrection"; "Even so reckon ye also yourselves to be dead unto sin, but alive unto God in Christ Jesus" (Rom. 6.5, 11). We depend on the death and resurrection of the Lord for our salvation; likewise, we depend on His death and resurrection for our daily victory.

The Lord Jesus has already accomplished full salvation—be it salvation to the sinners or to the believers—and all we need to do is to receive it by faith for it to become ours. We must know this Lord who died and has been resurrected; we ought to join ourselves to His death and resurrection by faith.

Our Lord is "the first" since He is the Source of all things: He also is "the last" since He is the End of all things. As we review the story of our salvation we know it is the Lord who first calls us and not we who seek the Lord; it is He who first loves us and not we who love Him. Thus do we know Him as the first.

But then we may sometimes wonder, Now that we are saved, what will be the extent of His salvation? Suppose the Lord saves us just this much and no more, what will happen to us?—If the work of God stops right here with initial salvation and goes no further, what can we do?—Where will the salvation of God lead us to?—What will be our future? Or we may even ponder our situation on a much wider scale. As we read the Book of Genesis, we of course learn that God is the Creator and Source of all things. But we also read how later on the serpent slipped into the Garden of Eden, how man then fell, and that Adam and Eve were driven out of the same Garden. In addition, the way to the tree of life was guarded by cherubim with the flame of a sword which turned in every direction. And finally, we learn from the early Genesis account that the earth was cursed and death came into the world. Now in our understanding of how these things happened, how can we refrain from asking what the final result of these things will be? Here we see that God has made a beginning with this world, yet what will be its end?

To these questions God himself gives the answer. The Book of Revelation, in fact, is God's answer. In the very first chapter we have this declaration by the Lord: "I am the first and the last." This is the revelation of Jesus Christ. And in the last chapter of this Book He again declares: "I am the Alpha and Omega, the first and the last, the beginning and the end" (22.13). This too is the revelation of Jesus Christ. In other words, what God has begun, He will in truth finish; what has not been solved earlier in the Garden of Eden, He will solve later on. His redemption is perfect and complete; and His eternal plan must be accomplished. All the problems which we cannot resolve today, He will definitely solve in the coming day. Thank God, one day Christ will conclude all things because He is the last just as He is the first. This, then, is the revelation of Jesus Christ. God shows us that this One who is the first and the last is indeed the answer to all questions.

"And the Living one"—We read in John's Gospel: "In him was life" (1.4); and also, Jesus' words: "I am the resurrection, and the life" (11.25). These passages show that Christ is the Source of life. His life is the uncreated life, He is eternally self-existing. He is the One who lives forever. He is the life.

"And I was dead"—Our Lord did in fact once become dead. On the one hand He died as a substitute for sinners. It was a case of "the righteous [dying] for the unrighteous" (1 Peter 3.18). On the other hand, through His death He released His life. How marvelous is this death!

"And, behold, I am alive for evermore"—Christ has risen from the dead. Innumerable people encounter death and die. Yet none has ever come back; no one by his own power has ever been resurrected. Indeed, during these thousands of years of human history millions and billions of people have passed away. "To go and not to return" seems to have been the unchanging rule since we have not seen any ever come back. Yet God allowed our Lord Jesus to die that through death He might prove His victory over death.

He did become dead, but now He is alive forever. How great is this declaration: "I am alive for ever-more"! At the time of Pentecost the apostle Peter unequivocally declared: "[Jesus] God raised up, having loosed the pangs of death: because it was not possible that he should be holden of it" (Acts 2.24). Death could not hold Him because death *has* no power to hold Him. The resurrection life can endure death. Though dead, now resurrected—this very fact of history proves how Christ's life can endure death and is able to pass through death. Many encounter something unpleasant and immediately feel as though they are meeting up with death. But this resurrection life of the Lord Jesus is not afraid to die. By passing through death it proves its power to outlive death. Resurrection life is that which can pass through death and still live. Whatever passes through death but is finished is *not* resurrection life.

The Lord instructed John to write to the angel of the church in Smyrna, saying that the One "who was dead and lives again" had a message for them because the church in Smyrna was one that had suffered greatly for the Lord and she had been faithful even to death. And thus did He use this kind of word to comfort her. Just as the gates of Hades could not prevail against Christ, so the gates of Hades cannot prevail against the church. If a church knows what resurrection is, she can withstand any trial and tribulation; for resurrection life is a life that endures death and can pass through death and rise up again. Hallelujah!

Our Lord once became dead, but He now is alive! Death has no power over Him!

The Lord is not only "alive"—He is also "for evermore"! He died only once, and He also was resurrected but once. After He was raised from the dead, He thereafter lives forever. He now exhibits not only the glory which He had with the Father before the world was (John 17.5) but also the added "glory of man." He ever lives—and not just for His own self but for us too: because "he ever liveth to make intercession for them" and He now "appears before the face of God for us" (Heb. 7.25, 9.24). Did he not say to His disciples, "Because I live, ye shall live also" (John 14.19)? And are not these words spoken to us too?

Knowing the Lord Jesus as the God who lives forever enables us to sense the presence of the Lord unceasingly in our spirit. Nothing strengthens us more than this sense of the Lord's actual presence. This is not a kind of emotional, imaginative, or psychological lift. Abraham, for example, knew God deeply after many years of following Him, and hence he "planted a tamarisk tree in Beer-sheba, and called there on the name of Jehovah, the *Everlasting God*" (Gen. 21.36). Daniel was known as the "servant of the living God"; and when he was thrown into the lions' den, his God shut the lions' mouths and they did not hurt him (Dan. 6.20,22).

George Muller once said: "If you walk with God, expecting Him to give you seasonal help, you will find that the living God will never fail you." An elderly brother who had known the living God for forty-four years once testified that God had never failed him. Whether in great tribulations, under heavy trials, or beset by deep poverty and many needs, God had never failed him. Because by grace he could trust God, this brother always received help in season. And for this he would gladly declare God's name.

Alexander Maclaren has told the following story concerning the greatest religious reformer in Germany: "Once Martin Luther felt that his future was full of dangers, and hence his heart was filled with sorrow and fear. He knew at the time that unless he could lay hold of the power from on high, he would not be able to get through. As Luther sat alone in his room, he used his finger to draw these words on the table: 'He is alive for evermore!' God is alive! Luther became joyful and his faith was restored." "He is alive for evermore" is always our strength and our hope. People will all pass away, yet only He exists forever.

Men are like lighted lamps; sooner or later they as flickering lights will be extinguished; Christ, though, is the True Light, the Source of all lights, who continues forevermore. Let us take encouragement and comfort in the fact that the living God whom Abraham called upon, Daniel served, George Muller trusted, and Martin Luther knew is also the God to whom we belong and serve. We ought to fall to the ground and worship. We ought to be filled with joy and to praise His name!

Yet there is more! The Lord not only "is alive for evermore," He also "has the keys of death and of Hades"—This tells us that all the things in the after-

life are in the Lord's hands. Death is joined with
Hades (note that the "Hades" mentioned here is not
"hell" or "the lake of fire"; in Hebrew it is *Sheol*, in
Greek it is *Hades*, and it means "the invisible
world"). In Revelation 6.8 it is said that Hades
follows death. In Revelation 20.14 we see that both
Hades and death end up in being cast into the Lake of
Fire. In these two passages just cited it would seem
that both Hades and death have taken up personality.
This would appear to be confirmed by such Scripture
passages as Hebrews 2.14 which says the devil has the
power of death and Matthew 16.18 which mentions
the gates (or powers) of Hades. Behind death and
Hades there is a personal devil who holds the power.
But our Lord has risen from the dead. Over Him
death and Hades have no more power; quite the contrary, He holds the keys of both. Here we see that far
from death and Hades holding power over our Lord,
the Latter has in fact overcome them!

Thank God that on the great day of resurrection
there "shall come to pass the saying that is written,
Death is swallowed up in victory" (1 Cor. 15.54). At
that time, all who belong to the Lord will boast, saying, "O death, where is thy victory? O death, where is
thy sting?" (v.55) Oh do let us realize that what we
are waiting for is not death. On the contrary, what we
are waiting for is the morning—the morning of resurrection. And for this reason we can wait with hope.

Yet the glorious Christ thus revealed to John is
not simply for the purpose of letting His servant
know what kind of Lord He is; it is in addition for the
sake of entrusting to His servant John a great and

important responsibility. This we see in the last two verses which comprise the first chapter of Revelation: "Write therefore the things which thou sawest, and the things which are, and the things which shall come to pass hereafter; the mystery of the seven stars which thou sawest in my right hand, and the seven golden candlesticks. The seven stars are the angels of the seven churches: and the seven candlesticks are seven churches" (vv.19-20). The Lord wants John to "write . . . the things which thou sawest, and the things which are, and the things which shall come to pass hereafter"—that is, He wants to leave a testimony in writing. He therefore commands John to write in order to complete the record of what He does on earth.

"The things which thou sawest"—This refers to what John has just seen, which is the vision of the glorious Christ. "The things which are" has reference to the things that are still present, which point to the church age, for the Lord later on states that "the seven stars *are* the angels of the seven churches: and the seven candlesticks *are* seven churches"—From this we see that the verb used here is "are" which in the original Greek is cast in the present tense; and hence this verb "are" ties in this verse 1.20b with the phrase "the things which are" spoken of in the preceding verse 19. Therefore the phrase "the things which are" alludes to the things of the church.

Let us now attempt to give some meaning to the seven stars and the seven golden candlesticks. The seven stars and the seven golden candlesticks are a mystery. Being a mystery, they not only involve physical substance but also have spiritual significance. Unless God reveals, no man can understand the mysteries in the Bible. But with God's revelation, mysteries are no longer things unknowable (Dan. 2.28, also 2.18–23). Here the mystery of the seven stars and the seven golden candlesticks has already been explained to John by the Lord. Let us apprehend it with a quiet spirit.

The Lord holds in His right hand the seven stars. This indicates that the Lord has full authority over the representatives of heavenly lights and that these representatives must bear their responsibilities in the churches where they are located. The right hand of the Lord—that powerful right hand—alone enables the stars to shine according to His will. It is also this powerful right hand of the Lord which alone can hold and keep these stars.

"Seven stars"—To what do they point? The Lord explains them to John by saying that "the seven stars are the angels of the seven churches." Who, then, are these "angels" here mentioned? Commentators have offered varied explanations. First of all, let us point out that these angels do not refer to angels in heaven, since they are angels among men. John wrote to the angels of the seven churches. If that is so, then it is obvious that John is *not* writing to the angels in heaven. Hence these angels must have reference not to those in heaven but to certain people in the churches.

What class of people in the seven churches are the angels of the seven churches? The basic definition of the Greek word translated "angel" (or "messenger") means one who is being sent. Thus angels or messengers are the representatives of the churches.

As we closely study Revelation chapters 2 and 3 we shall readily discover that the Lord treats these "angels" as the responsible ones in those seven churches. In this connection, let us take note of the Lord's words spoken to these various churches. He warns the church in Ephesus: ". . . or else I come to thee, and will remove thy candlestick out of its place, except thou repent." He reprimands the church in Pergamum: "Thou hast there some that hold the teaching of Balaam . . . So hast thou also some that hold the teaching of the Nicolaitans in like manner." He denounces the church in Thyatira: "Thou sufferest the woman Jezebel, who callest herself a prophetess; and she teacheth and seduceth my servants to commit fornication, and to eat things sacrificed to idols." He reminds the church in Sardis: "Be thou watchful, and establish the things that remain, which were ready to die . . . If therefore thou shalt not watch, I will come as a thief, and thou shalt not know what hour I will come upon thee." He encourages the church in Philadelphia: "Hold fast that which thou hast." And He counsels the church in Laodicea: "I counsel thee to buy of me gold refined by fire . . . and white garments that thou mayest clothe thyself . . . and eyesalve to anoint thine eyes . . ." Now all of the above words are spoken by the Lord to the churches (cf. Rev. 1.11, 2.7). Yet the letters themselves are all written to the angels (or messengers) belonging to these churches. This fully suggests that the Lord wants these angels to be aware of the conditions of the churches where they are and to take up their respective responsibilities as they ought.

Since the meaning of the word "angels" is those who are sent, there are in fact always a few representing the one who sends them. A good example of this observation is found in the very words of our Lord Jesus when He was on the earth: "He that receiveth you receiveth me," said the Lord Jesus to His disciples, "and he that receiveth me receiveth him that sent me" (Matt. 10.40). Hence these angels mentioned in Revelation chapters 1 to 3 must be men in the seven churches who are gifted and have learned spiritually so that they can influence and modify the churches. We do not know what their positions and works in the churches are, but they each must be the nucleus of these seven churches—people with spiritual weight, to each of whom the Lord entrusts the responsibility of the whole church which is in that one's care.

Judging from the contents of these seven letters, it is evident that these angels and the churches where they are cannot be separated. For example, in chapter 1.11 we read: "What thou seest, write in a book and send it to the seven churches"; while at the beginning of each letter recorded in chapters 2 and 3 it is always introduced by: "To the angel of the church in . . ." This shows that the particular church and pertinent angel are inseparable. Moreover, these seven letters are written to the seven angels of the seven churches, and in each letter there are such words as: "He that hath an ear, let him hear what the Spirit saith to the churches.'' This indicates that the Lord treats the angels as the churches for He holds them responsible for the things in the churches where they are. Nevertheless, all this does not mean that the angel and the church are exactly the same. For example, to some of the churches the Lord is found saying such things as the following: ''The devil is about to cast some of you into prison'' (2.10); ''even in the days of Antipas my witness, my faithful one, who was killed among you'' (2.13); ''Thou hast there some that hold the teaching of Balaam'' (2.14); ''to the rest that are in Thyatira'' (2.24); and ''Thou hast a few names in Sardis that did not defile their garments'' (3.4). Because the Lord in these statements separates or singles out some of the brethren from among the rest in the various assemblies, this would seem to indicate that the angels are different from the churches.

Now the Lord uses stars to represent these angels. Hence they must have heavenly positions—like the stars in heaven—and have heavenly-type experiences. They bear witness to the Lord and shine for Him like the light of the stars at night. Their aspiration and joy are heavenly in nature, not earthly. They have intimate fellowship with Christ, and they also receive the power and authority of the Lord because they are in His right hand. These messengers represent the churches since they are the most faithful ones in these churches. They are occupied with the things of the churches, and they look upon the success or failure of the churches as their own success or failure. These whom the Lord has sent are those who willingly bear the responsibility of the churches.

Therefore, whoever expects to be useful in the Lord's hand must often kneel before God and pray for the church with tears and a poured-out soul. In spite of the fact that others' defeat is not their defeat, nevertheless, if they do not care about the defeat of others, it will be reckoned by God as indeed their defeat. These responsible ones should have largeness of heart to embrace all the children of God, caring for the affairs of others as for their own. Otherwise, they will sadden the Lord's heart as well as endanger themselves. How pathetic if this should happen! On the other hand, if people genuinely commit themselves wholly into the Lord's hand and joyfully bear the burdens of the churches for His sake, they will not only accomplish great works for the Lord but also receive rewards from Him.

We further need to recognize that the Lord is most fair in His judgment. When He observed faithfulness in the church in Smyrna and in the church in Philadelphia, He commended them. But to the other five churches He had words of reprimand or correction for each one. Although the angels represent the church and they are as stars having their spiritual responsibilities, there is a distinction between the angels and the churches just as stars are distinct from candlesticks. At the time of judgment God will judge those with responsibility as well as the churches in general according to their respective works, for "to whomsoever much is given, of him much shall be required" (Luke 12.48). The Lord knows who are His and who are faithful to the end.

In this connection it is worth noticing that the

words which the Lord speaks to His churches (including warnings as well as judgments) are directed to the angels as well as to the churches. The churches have the possibility of being defeated; but then, so are the angels subject to possible defeat. Ah, even the stars—the angels or messengers—that are held in the right hand of the Lord may fail, even to the degree of: "Thou hast a name that thou livest, and thou art dead" (3.1) or, "Behold, I [the Lord] stand at the door and knock" (3.20). How serious a matter this is! In the light of this sobering thought, anyone who is greatly used by the Lord or who bears heavy responsibility in the church must not be proud, unwatchful, or unfaithful.

"The seven candlesticks," explains the Lord, "are seven churches"—Concerning these seven churches represented by the seven candlesticks, we must recognize three different approaches to a fuller understanding of this Bible passage: (1) that these seven churches were actual churches in those days; (2) that these seven churches typify the seven stages of church history in general; and (3) that the conditions prevailing in these seven churches have been simultaneously present in all seven stages of general church history.

We can safely conclude from the words "John to the seven churches that are in Asia" (1.4) that these seven letters written by the apostle were sent to seven churches which actually existed in those days. Furthermore, "The things which are" that the Lord alluded to as recorded in Revelation 1.19 must refer to these seven churches and the various conditions pertaining to them which are cited in the seven letters of chapters 2 and 3. For when the Lord says "which are," these things concerning the seven churches must have been present as actual things in those days. Let us not think that the Lord would not come back until the conditions of these seven churches had gradually turned or developed into the seven periods of general church history. For we must carefully note that the Lord definitely spoke to His churches such words as this: "That which ye have, hold fast till I come" and "Be thou watchful . . . If therefore thou shalt not watch, I will come as a thief" (2.25, 3.2–3). These statements plainly tell us that there was certainly a possibility of the Lord's coming back at that time.

On the other hand we must not overlook the fact that there were more churches than just these seven at that time. Certainly those in that day that needed such teaching, warning, and encouragement were more in number than simply these seven churches. For instance, would not such a notable church as the one in Antioch also receive a letter like these? Is there not therefore a deeper meaning in the fact that out of the many churches which were then existing the Lord chose these particular seven churches to receive His special admonitions? As we look at the conditions of these seven churches taken as a whole, we come to understand that the Lord sovereignly chose these seven churches in order to express His will regarding the church of all periods. He will use these seven churches to disclose the conditions of the church after the apostolic age and up until the time of His return.

In the original Greek language, there is no article placed before the words "seven churches" in the pertinent sentence found in Revelation 1.20c, thus strongly hinting that what the Lord says here does not point singularly to these seven churches but instead to all the churches which they represent. For "seven" in the Bible is a perfect number; and thus these seven churches can represent all the churches. Were these seven candlesticks meant only to refer to these seven churches, then what must have been the state of the churches at that time other than these seven churches and those churches that were to come afterwards?

Furthermore, in the letters ordered by the Lord to be written by John to the angels of the seven churches, each of them contains the injunction: "He that hath an ear, let him hear what the Spirit saith to the churches." This clearly indicates that these letters were not aimed only at the seven churches actually existing during that time but were also for all other saints everywhere who might have ears to hear the word of the Lord. Consequently, in view of all these evidences, the seven churches here symbolized by the seven candlesticks must be representative of all the churches on earth.

Now our Lord has not explicitly stated anywhere that these seven churches typify the churches at large in each period of church history. This is probably to induce us to be ever watchful since we do not know the hour of His coming (cf. Mark 13.35). Though these seven churches do signify prophetically the general history of the church on earth, nothing is specified that Smyrna will arise only after Ephesus has passed, or that Pergamum will come only after Smyrna has disappeared, and so forth. According to the general conditions to be found in church history, the first period of that history bears a resemblance to the conditions which prevailed in the church at Ephesus; the second period, a resemblance to that of the church at Smyrna, etc. Nevertheless, even during the period when the church at Ephesus existed, there were also present the conditions of the other six churches—except that the conditions of the church at Ephesus were more predominant. Likewise, during the period when there existed the church at Smyrna, the conditions prevailing in the other six churches were present too—but with the state of the church at Smyrna more prevailing. Hence in every period of church history all the various conditions of the churches are present, just as was the case of the seven churches that coexisted together in their day.

Now the Lord said to the angel of the church in Thyatira: "Nevertheless that which ye have, hold fast till I come" (2.25); to the angel of the church in Sardis He declared: "I will come as a thief" and, "thou shalt not know what hour I will come upon thee" (3.3); and to the angel of the church in Philadelphia the Lord warned: "I come quickly" (3.11). To these three churches the Lord mentions His coming—thus allowing for the presumption that all three with their particular characteristics will continue on until His return. The church in Laodicea is the last church listed, so that naturally it should continue to exist with the above three until the Lord's return. Inasmuch as the Lord speaks about His coming to the three churches in Thyatira, Sardis, and Philadelphia, time-wise that event should get closer and closer. In fact His words betray such a progression. To the church in Thyatira, for instance, He says "till I come"—as if His coming is still quite distant. To the church in Sardis, though, the Lord declares, "I will come upon thee"—implying that His coming is more definite. And to the church in Philadelphia, He states: "I come quickly"—as though wishing to show that His coming is imminent. It is for this reason that the church must be watchful and prepared to meet her Lord.

Hence the last four of these seven churches with their particular traits will continue on till the time of the Lord's coming. This is not meant to signify, however, that these four were to be raised up simultaneously and to continue on together till the coming of the Lord. The church of Thyatira is raised up, then the church in Sardis is raised up, followed by the church in Philadelphia, and after that the church in Laodicea. The ones raised up earlier among these four will not disappear when the later ones arrive; rather, they all are to exist until the Lord's return. In other words, their being raised up is at different times but their termination shall all happen at the same time.

At the very outset we mentioned that the main purpose in our studying the Book of Revelation is to know who Jesus Christ is. If we therefore have any ambition in spiritual things, that ambition is to be one and one only—namely, to seek to know the Lord with those who also know Him. But knowing the Lord is not an empty word. No one who truly knows Him will fail to fall at His feet. And only he who prostrates himself before the Lord shall be entrusted by Him with spiritual responsibility. Let me then ask you, How about *your* knowing the Lord? What is *your* burden for the church of God? If you are faithful, and hold on to what you have, and stand firm in faith, you shall shine as the stars of heaven and shall become useful vessels in the Lord's right hand.

5 | Four New Testament Ministers

And straightway in the synagogues he proclaimed Jesus, that he is the Son of God. And all that heard him were amazed, and said, Is not this he that in Jerusalem made havoc of them that called on this name? and he had come hither for this intent, that he might bring them bound before the chief priests. But Saul increased the more in strength, and confounded the Jews that dwelt at Damascus, proving that this is the Christ. And when many days were fulfilled, the Jews took counsel together to kill him: but their plot became known to Saul. And they watched the gates also day and night that they might kill him: but his disciples took him by night, and let him down through the wall, lowering him in a basket. And when he was come to Jerusalem, he assayed to join himself to the disciples: and they were all afraid of him, not believing that he was a disciple. But Barnabas took him, and brought him to the apostles, and declared unto them how he had seen the Lord in the way, and that he had spoken to him, and how at Damascus he had preached boldly in the name of Jesus. And he was with them going in and going out at Jerusalem. (Acts 9.20–28)

And walking by the sea of Galilee, he saw two brethren, Simon who is called Peter, and Andrew his brother, casting a net into the sea; for they were fishers. And he saith unto them, Come ye after me, and I will make you fishers of men. And they straightway left the nets, and followed him. And going on from thence he saw two other brethren, James the son of Zebedee, and John his brother, in the boat with Zebedee their father, mending their nets; and he called them. And they straightway left the boat and their father, and followed him. (Matt. 4.18–22)

And he put all things in subjection under his feet, and gave him to be head over all things to the church, which is his body, the fulness of him that filleth all in all. (Eph. 1.22–23)

In whom ye also are builded together for a habitation of God in the Spirit. (Eph. 2.22)

If ye have tasted that the Lord is gracious: unto whom coming, a living stone, rejected indeed of men, but with God elect, precious, ye also, as living stones, are built up a spiritual house, to be a holy priesthood, to offer up spiritual sacrifices, acceptable to God through Jesus Christ. (1 Peter 2.3–5)

I write unto you, my little children, because your sins are forgiven you for his name's sake. I write unto you, fathers, because ye know him who is from the beginning. I write unto you, young men, because ye have overcome the evil one. I have written unto you, little children, because ye know the Father. (1 John 2.12–13)

Verily, verily, I say unto thee, When thou wast young, thou girdedst thyself, and walkedst whither thou wouldest: but when thou shalt be old, thou shalt stretch forth thy hands, and another shall gird thee, and carry thee whither thou wouldest not. . . . Peter therefore seeing him saith to Jesus, Lord, and what shall this man do? (John 21.18,21)

And when they had appointed him a day, they came to him into his lodging in great number; to whom he expounded the matter, testifying the kingdom of God, and persuading them concerning Jesus, both from the law of Moses and from the prophets, from morning till evening. (Acts 28.23)

This thou knowest, that all that are in Asia turned away from me; of whom are Phygelus and Hermogenes. (2 Tim. 1.15)

But there arose false prophets also among the people, as among you also there shall be false teachers, who shall privily bring in destructive heresies, denying even the Master that bought them, bringing upon themselves swift destruction. (2 Peter 2.1)

Beloved, believe not every spirit, but prove the spirits, whether they are of God; because many false prophets are gone out into the world. (1 John 4.1)

For many deceivers are gone forth into the world, even they that confess not that Jesus Christ cometh in the flesh. (2 John 7a)

The meaning of the word "minister" (*diakonos*) in the original New Testament Greek applies not only to the deacons in the church but also to all else who serve. All who serve God and the gospel are ministers. So that when, as we are shortly to do, we mention four ministers, we mean four servants (or workers) of the Lord. In the above Scripture readings we can distinguish four distinct lines of ministry. These four lines of ministry form an outline of the New Testament. And we call those who pioneer these four lines, the four ministers.

One special feature we cannot fail to notice in the Gospels is the fact that among the Lord's twelve disciples, three are quite frequently with Him. I believe we all know that they are James, Peter, and John. Together these three saw the Lord transformed on the mount, went with Him into the house of Jairus, and finally were closest to the Lord in the Garden of Gethsemane. Why from among the Twelve did the Lord especially choose these three disciples? Why did He give them a more prominent place? One very significant reason was that God called them in order to establish three distinctive lines of New Testament ministry. Yet these three lines, as it turned out, were incomplete; for as we look into the Book of Acts we immediately notice that the Lord brought in still another person besides these three men. Now was this other person Matthias? It must be said that although Matthias was indeed chosen to be an apostle by the casting of lots, nevertheless he was not the man. No, this distinction fell to another, even to the beloved brother Paul, who was likewise specially chosen by the Lord.

In the New Testament can be found many people who work for the Lord, but those who stand out conspicuously are only four in number. And these four ought to be listed in the following manner: first, James; second, Peter; third, Paul; and fourth, John. This, I believe, is the proper Scriptural order commonly accepted by most Bible students. And although we may not be able to exhaust the deepest meaning of these four lines of ministry, we can at least come to know something about them. A glimpse of them—however dim it may be—can help us in our Christian walk on earth.

First, James

James is the least conspicuous among the four. He has not written any book. The New Testament book called James was not written by him but by the James who was one of the Lord's brothers according to the flesh. Both Peter and John are most zealous and active; and they have left to us monumental records of their endeavors. James, however, does not appear to have done anything special. On the contrary, he seems to have been a very hidden man. Why, then, would the Lord have chosen him to represent a distinctive line of New Testament ministry? How could he ever be ranked among the four?

Let us see that what James represents is not the gifts of preaching, healing, and wonders. These gifts are good, yet they are not James' specialty. What, then, does he represent? We must recognize that he performed the greatest as well as the most exceptional work of all, which was, that he became the first martyr among the apostles (see Acts 12.1f.). The most special and significant of the four lines of ministry is that of suffering. Despite the distinctives peculiarly found in the works of Peter, Paul, and John, there is nonetheless one thing they *all* had in common, which was this element of suffering—for suffering constitutes one of the basics of a Christian.

Today many love to read the excellent letters of Paul, to hear of the great works of Peter, and to learn of the wonderful visions of John, but they altogether forget about this servant James. Yet how can we overlook the fact that all works of God are based on what James represents? Though a Peter may lead 3,000 people to Christ in one day and a Paul is able to establish churches everywhere, nevertheless, if there is not the suffering of James, the Lord will not be satisfied. For in His very coming into this world, our Lord Jesus stood in the place of the rejected. And if we therefore do not suffer with Him—and no matter what good works we may perform—we cannot satisfy His heart.

Why does the Lord so conceal—yes, even seem to bury—this man James? It is because He aims at projecting the specialty of James upon our senses by means of casting this specialty in stark relief. To illustrate what we mean, let us say that in a room we have many chairs along with some lamps and tables. We are so used to them that we do not think of them at all. Suppose, however, that one day all these objects are removed except for one tiny table. I believe that whoever comes into the room thereafter will without exception notice this tiny table. When many items are gathered, no single one of them is particularly noticeable; but if all be taken away except one, this remaining item will become very conspicuous. In like manner, the Lord hides all the gifts which James possesses except this special one of suffering in order to project this remaining gift into greater prominence. Peter himself once declared (and this is what the Bible says), "Forasmuch then as Christ suffered in the flesh, arm ye yourselves also with the same mind" (1 Peter 4.1). Only by suffering can we overcome all things and complete the eternal purpose of God.

Please allow me to speak with great frankness here that those who are not willing to suffer with Christ should not expect to be exalted with Him, for only those who have suffered are worthy to be lifted up (cf. Rom. 8.17). We must follow in the footsteps of James.

There are many other truths to be gleaned from the life of James which can help us, but we must move on to the other three ministries.

Second, Peter

Before we deal with what Peter represents, we ought to look first at the individual characteristics belonging to the lines of ministry of Peter, Paul, and John respectively. Though these traits will not be treated systematically, our brief treatment may nonetheless help in understanding them better.

The works of Peter and Paul are very different. In reading the Gospel according to Mark, the Gospel according to Luke, and the Book of Acts, we can easily discern the difference (Mark, it should be noted, received much from Peter, whereas Luke followed Paul in his presentation). The testimony which Peter gave on the Day of Pentecost differs in emphasis from the testimony given by Paul. They cannot be mixed up. Moreover, the work of John seems to stand all by itself: the gift or testimony he received from the Lord is quite different from those of Peter and Paul.

What is Peter's testimony? In reading Matthew 16 and Acts 2 we can readily recognize that what Peter is particularly concerned with is *the kingdom of God.* His line of ministry is especially focused on that. What about Paul? I trust all who have read the entire writings of Paul have seen that what he puts forth is none other than *the house of God.* In other words, it is the church of God. All the testimonies and works of Paul's entire life are centered on this point. And finally, John's testimony is different from these two. For example, he never talks about church affairs. Although Peter himself does not speak specifically on the church, nor touch on its organization, he at least mentions something about the elders. John, however, is completely silent on such church affairs as appointments and organization. He talks almost exclusively about the fathers, the young men, and the children. What this signifies with respect to John is a testimony concerning the *family of God.*

Consequently, three very distinctive lines of ministry are presented to us: (1) Peter—the kingdom of God; (2) Paul—the house of God; and (3) John—the family of God. If we can clearly grasp these three lines, we will receive more light from God. This does not imply, of course, that Peter never mentions what John does, since obviously Peter does touch a little upon the family of God. But his principal subject is always the kingdom of God. In a simliar way, Paul is also found talking a little about the affairs of God's family, with John likewise speaking sometimes on the things of God's kingdom: yet the central theme of Paul is always the church of God and that of John is always the family of God. To sum up, then, we may say that although these three lines are not absolute, each of them forms a predominant strain within each of these three men's ministries.

Of these three lines of ministry, the one identified with Peter marks the beginning. The first person to speak for Christianity is this apostle of Christ, while the last one to speak is John (the latter's Book of Revelation is the last of the 66 books of the Bible to be written). What about Paul? He stands between Peter and John and thus succeeds the one who is before him (Peter) and passes on to the other who is after him (John). What God sets forth in the Bible (and in this order) are the kingdom of God, the house of God, and the family of God.

How very tragic it is today that so many people know nothing about the kingdom of God and the family of God, and are equally ignorant concerning the house of God. All they know about are human organizations and denominations. Whenever they are asked what the differentiations are among the kingdom, family, and house of God, they will more likely answer that these are almost the same. They deem entering the church to be the same as entering the family of God as well as entering His kingdom. They have no idea that there are vast differences among these three. Because of this, God needs a Peter, a Paul, and a John to substantiate His kingdom, His house, and His family.

That the Lord grants the keys of the kingdom of heaven to Peter confirms the fact that this apostle will do the work of opening doors—first to the Jews and then to the Gentiles. Since the keys of the kingdom of heaven are in Peter's hand, he must of necessity be one who has himself already entered the kingdom of heaven. For the keys are committed to Peter's hand for him to keep. If, for example, the key to the gate opening upon Wen teh Li* has been given into my hand for keeping, people who come early to our meeting will have to wait outside the iron gate till I arrive and open it with the key. I will enter in first and afterwards other people can come in. It is simply impossible for anyone *without* the key to enter first. Hence it is crystal clear that Peter is the first one who enters the realm of the kingdom of heaven.

The word which our Lord spoke to Peter in Matthew 16 is most amazing. How did He phrase it? "Upon this rock I will build my church . . . I will give unto thee the keys of the kingdom of heaven" (vv.18-19). Can we detect the point of difference in this verse? Here is a great turning point: The Lord gives the keys of the kingdom of heaven to Peter so

---

*The name of the lane where is located the building in which the saints at Shanghai, China, met for a long time.—*Translator*

that the latter is now responsible for the kingdom to the extent that he may manipulate the timing of the opening of the kingdom of heaven. As regards the church, though, the Lord says this: "Upon this rock *I* will build my church." The Lord himself will build, and He allows no one to touch the church.

Here marks the distinctive difference between the kingdom of heaven and the church. What is the kingdom of heaven? It is the spiritual realm of God on earth. The kingdom of heaven demonstrates the sovereignty and rule of God. The house of God, though, expresses God's character, how glorious and loving and righteous it is. And the family of God manifests the love of God and the relationship between Him and us.

These three aspects—the kingdom, the house, and the family of God—are each complete in itself and the three of them should not be mixed up. How many of God's people lump all within the one church aspect—saying that this belongs to the church and that also belongs to the church. They make the church a warehouse which stores up everything. Such thinking merely reveals how lacking is the understanding of the truths of the Bible.

Peter bears witness to the kingdom. He opens the gate that all may go in. In this connection, what does the Lord say in John 3? "Verily, verily, I say unto thee, Except one be born of water and the Spirit, he cannot enter into the kingdom of God" (v.5). If we were to utter this verse, we most likely would set it forth in this fashion: "Except one be born of water and the Spirit, he cannot enter the house of God"!

But, no, it is the kingdom of God. All who would enter the kingdom must be born again, for it is the born-again ones alone who may enter. The keys which Peter used on the Day of Pentecost are these: repentance and baptism. And hence three thousand entered the kingdom of God on that day. And this marked the beginning of the kingdom of God. Many people maintain that the church commenced at Pentecost. This is indeed true, but let it not be forgotten that the kingdom of God also commenced at Pentecost. What Peter touched on later in his epistles concerning salvation, reward, and so forth are all related to the kingdom to come, and they are not in any way in conflict with the entry into the kingdom of God at Pentecost.

Was the work done at Pentecost enough? Certainly not, for God again sent Peter—this time to the house of Cornelius. On the Day of Pentecost Peter opened the gate and many *Jews* entered the kingdom of God. On this second occasion the Lord directed Peter to open the gate of the kingdom to the Gentiles, thus fulfilling the Lord's words recorded in Matthew 8: "And I say unto you, that many shall come from the east and the west, and shall sit down with Abraham, and Isaac, and Jacob, in the kingdom of heaven" (v.11). Yet even before Peter had opened the gate so that the Gentiles might receive grace, God had already begun to prepare another man—Paul. Accordingly, the work of Peter, if judged from the view of dispensation, ended with the house of Cornelius. Although he still continued to bear much witness, his work—so far as the character of the time was concerned—was already finished. How marvelous was this divine arrangement: Peter went to the house of Cornelius during the time of Acts chapter 10, yet Paul had already repented by the time of Acts chapter 9.

You will recall that Paul was one who had formerly persecuted the Lord with great fervor. On the road to Damascus, though, he was enlightened by the Lord and was graciously saved. His eyes, however, were not opened until the Lord sent Ananias to him, who told him that he was a chosen vessel to God. This word from Ananias revealed the mind of the Lord: for although the kingdom of God is great and many have been brought in through Peter, it now needed someone to begin to set things in order. So the Lord raised up Paul and used him as a chosen vessel. The word of Ananias was well spoken. The very first thing he said was, "Brother Saul"—thus demonstrating that all enmities had been cleared away. Only then could Paul testify for the Lord and become effective in service.

Subsequently we find Paul extending his work from within the city of Damascus to outside the city. The sphere of his work began to expand. Yet how did he get down the city wall and escape from Damascus? Interestingly, Paul was let down the wall by some of the disciples who were there. Though he could have climbed down the wall himself, he refused to do that. He would rather be lowered by the disciples. This bespeaks fellowship, help, and approval of the brethren. So that Paul did not launch out singly; he had the sympathy and support of other people. How much more effective *our* works will be if there are people behind us praying and helping us. And when Paul arrived at Jerusalem, he was at first shunned by the disciples there, who doubted his conversion; later on, though, through the introduction of Barnabas he was able to go in and out among the disciples, his fellowship with them having become full and complete and void of any hindrance. In this way he was soon to commence the continuation of Peter's work.

Now let us return to Peter. When the Lord called him to the house of Cornelius he was at first reluctant to go to this Gentile home. The Lord therefore gave him a vision. In that vision Peter observed descending towards him from heaven a certain large vessel, as it were a great sheet. And inside the sheet were all manner of four-footed beasts and creeping things of the earth and birds of the heaven—but no fish. Why— since beasts, creeping things, birds, and fishes are all commonly known and seen—are the common fishes not mentioned? This is because, in accordance with what the ark of Noah typifies, there is no instance mentioned in the account of the Flood of the saving of fish. Since fishes are not included among all other creatures saved through the ark, they are likewise not included in the vision given to Peter.

What is the meaning of the great sheet with the four-footed beasts and creeping things and birds? Let us realize that this vessel similar in appearance to a great sheet represents the work and ministry of Peter. It is not really a vessel commonly understood, nor is it something like a boat that has a definite dimension: it is a great sheet, and a sheet does not have a fixed form, for it is something which has not been made into a particular shape or figure but is still considered a raw piece of material. Now Peter's work is just that: he is concerned primarily with getting raw materials —with drawing people in. Who, then, will come in to shape these raw materials? It is Paul who shall come, and he will specialize in making something of these materials. It would seem as though Peter purchases the cloth and Paul works as a tailor. Peter's life work is therefore much like a sheet—limited and without too much form.

Let us next look at the three items found in this great sheet. Birds are active creatures. Sometimes they fly about very wildly. Sometimes they rest on treetops or housetops, sometimes they take a few hops here and there on the ground. They are most free in their movement and have absolutely no restraint. Hence they are the wildest. The beasts are ferocious and fearsome animals. And the creeping things, as we all know, point to uncleanness or filthiness. In the eyes of God, the Gentiles are nothing more than beasts, creeping things, or birds. But now He envelops all these wild and ferocious and unclean things within a great sheet. In a word, He puts us unbelievers in a new environment so that we are no longer wild and ferocious and unclean—and that is the gospel.

According to the Bible, there is only the gospel of the kingdom, there is no gospel of the church. By receiving the gospel people enter the kingdom of God as well as the church. We enter into a new realm, a new environment; we come under a new authority.

Formerly we were in the hand of Satan, but now we are in God's hand. And that is what is meant by being saved. To be saved means to be placed by God in a new position.

Today many magnify the church beyond measure, as though once entering the church one gets everything. They forget about the entering of the kingdom of God. For to be saved means not only entering the church but also the kingdom. To become children of God is to be given certain rights or authorities (John 1.12). Since to become God's child does not depend on what one is but on the authority which God gives to him, everyone may enter.

Therefore the work of bringing people from the outside in is the work of Peter. In other words, Peter's ministry is to lead people into the kingdom of God. And what is the kingdom of God? Quite simply, it is that realm which is under the authority and sovereignty of God. And to enter the kingdom therefore means *to become subject to the sovereignty of God.* So that Peter specializes in drawing in bundle upon bundle. Each drawing in of the sheet will add more citizens to the kingdom of God.

But as to what should be done to these bundles after having been drawn into the kingdom, that is not the main concern of Peter. It is left to Paul to take up such responsibility, because the work of Paul is to arrange and put into order those whom Peter has drawn into the kingdom. Can you at all find in Paul's letters the term "born again"? No, he talks about justification but never uses the term regeneration in the sense of a personal born-again experience. With Peter, however, he speaks a great deal about being born again. (Peter also mentions a great deal about inheritance, which subject Paul himself touches upon but seldom John if ever—since the latter's specialty is the family of God.)

In the Book of Acts much is said about the kingdom of God (even Paul mentions it), because at that time so many were being saved and drawn into the kingdom. Had we known on the day we were saved even a little of what they knew concerning the kingdom of God, we would be quite different today. Our current pitiable condition is in reality all of our own making, for we make self the center of everything and take the Lord merely as a helper to us. Indeed, God wants to bless us; but He desires even more greatly for us to enter His kingdom and to be *under His government.*

Oh let us all realize that salvation is not merely for enjoyment; it is preeminently to be placed under the sovereignty of God. Formerly we did what we liked and wasted away our days carelessly; now we are required to submit to God. Once we are saved we cannot afford to be careless. We must accept discipline. Salvation is none other than being put under the yoke of the Holy Spirit. If anyone wants to be saved, the Holy Spirit will place a yoke on that one. And whoever has this yoke upon him or her is saved. From the standpoint of the flesh, salvation is not at all pleasant because it brings the person under the sovereignty and government of God. And this, as we have seen, is clearly Peter's work and ministry. Whether it be ferocious beasts or unclean creeping

things or unruly birds, he bundles them together and
brings them into the kingdom of God.

Third, Paul

Paul is the one who succeeds the work of Peter.
For this reason, he calls himself a master builder—
one who builds the house. Many of us are aware that
all the teachings of Paul are consummated in his Letter to the Ephesians. And the theme of Ephesians is
the house of God. Whatever has been drawn in from
outside must now begin to be arranged and adorned.
The work of Paul is therefore the work of beautifying
along various lines.

Romans, for instance, speaks on justification, the
victorious life, and the life of obedience. These are
not the ways of entering the kingdom of God but are
the works of adornment—that is to say, the making
of improvements on the existing model. In his First
Letter to the Corinthians what Paul writes about is,
that once having submitted ourselves to God in His
kingdom, how are we to behave in various areas of
the Christian life? What Paul discusses there is our
conduct with respect to such matters as meetings, the
breaking of bread, marriage, receiving one another,
and having fellowship with the saints.

What this apostle is about can be likened to the
taking up of a pair of shears to cut up a sheet in order
to give it a definite shape and thus subject it to certain
restrictions. The things which are now in God's house
must be set in assigned places. Why? Because the nature of God is to be expressed through the house.

Whether a person is neat or sloppy can be judged by the state of that one's house, since the house reflects the personality of the owner. Nowhere is one's character more exposed and more revealed than in a person's house. Suppose, for example, that the books on your shelves are piled in a disorderly fashion, garbage is scattered everywhere on the floor, the bedding has been pushed aside without any folding, and the dust on the tables and chairs has been accumulating heavily. Your friend, upon entering your house and witnessing such a scene, will know immediately what sort of person you are. If you visit people in *their* houses, *your* true character may not be exposed. But everything in your *own* house will certainly reveal your true self, because it is your place of rest, the place where you live; therefore it will betray most distinctly and most fully your character and personality.

Hence the testimony which Peter gives will cause you to be a citizen of God's kingdom so that you may be subject to the mighty hand of God's sovereignty. Yet this apostle will not deal with any of the details, since that activity is not within the scope of his work and ministry and therefore does not require his attention. With Paul it is a different matter, for he has been charged by God to continue this work begun by Peter. Just look at Paul for a moment and see how precise he is. He mentions how husband and wife should love each other, how the brethren ought to care for one another, and so forth. All these concerns are related to the affairs of the house of God; they tell us what behavior is pleasing to God. Moreover, besides dealing with these more mundane affairs Paul also treats of such spiritual matters as meetings, baptism, gifts, the breaking of bread, and various ministries, as well as the order and structure in the church. Hence he can be likened to an interior decorator.

"In whom ye also are builded together for a habitation of God in the Spirit" (Eph. 2.22). This verse tells us explicitly that the church is the house of God. All believers are parts of the house, they being joined together to be one house. Each person is like a brick, a piece of wood, or a shingle. Only as all manifest the nature of God can they be fitly framed into the one house of God. And this is the line of ministry that the Lord had given to Paul.

Yet is the foundation work of Peter and the building ministry of Paul enough to satisfy the heart and mind of God? Can God's will be fully realized through just these two lines of ministry? No, there is still another man with another important line of ministry. And this we wish to look into next.

Fourth, John

John in almost all of his ministry treats of our relationship with God, with the result that he is concerned primarily with the affairs of God's family. His testimony is full of life, and hence he never dwells on anything external. Do you see anywhere in his letters that he writes on elderhood, taxation, or head covering? As regards individual conduct, John merely states that we should love one another—and that is

about all he says on the matter. To put it most suc-
cinctly, the testimony of John is confined to the Holi-
est of All—it is full of spiritual reality. He never
touches on outward things but is always speaking on
that which is *inward*, that is to say, the depths. Hence
the word "life" is seen a great deal in both his Gospel, his letters, and the Book of Revelation. The characteristic of his ministry is that of recovery after there
has been a general falling away or spiritual declension. For at the time he wrote his letters, his Gospel,
and Revelation, apostasy had become quite prevailing. There had arisen a number of false prophets and
false christs. People had even tried to overthrow the
kingdom of God and had come to consider the house
of God a matter of their personal domain. There had
developed a form of godliness but without its reality.

In view of this state of affairs, John stepped forward and spoke on the inner reality of things: which is
life. Men may overturn the kingdom of heaven and
the house, but they can never overturn life. For life always exists. Possessing this reality, everything will
turn out right. John's testimony is therefore concerned with the last days. He leads people to the innermost recess to discover what a God they really
have.

Let us now make a short analysis of these three
lines of ministry. It may be said in brief that Peter
speaks of a new realm—the kingdom of God; Paul,
of a new position—in the house of God; and John, of
a new relationship—that of a father to his son. How
extensively John, in his letters, deals with the fathers,

the young people, and the children. All of these are persons within God's family, and they are all interrelated. What is John aiming at? His aim is to see and arrive at the best possible progress or development in God's family. Paul speaks about the new position —how to obey God and to express His nature in the house of God. Accordingly, in the New Testament we can observe these three lines of ministry. If we want to find the line on the kingdom, read particularly the Gospel according to Matthew, the Gospel according to Mark, 1 and 2 Peter, and part of Hebrews. If we want to see the church as the house of God, nothing fuller and more complete can be found on this subject than the letters of Paul. The letters of John, however, deal almost exclusively with the family of God. Let me reiterate that these distinctions which have been drawn here are not absolute; they are only meant to show the respective emphases which are to be found in the ministries of these three servants of God.

The Beginning and the End

We will now see how these three lines of ministry had their beginning and how they ended. What was Peter doing when the Lord called him? He was at that time casting nets into the sea with his brother Andrew. How about John? He was in the boat mending the nets. Here we are witnessing a most amazing thing, in that when Peter and John were called, God had already arranged for them their respective work as exemplified in what occupied them when the Lord walked by and called them. For instance, when Peter was called, he was casting nets. So that later on, his ministry was the work of casting nets as a fisher of men. His was a front line work, much like that of a vanguard; for he was the first one who broke through to reach the Jews, and he was also the very first one who opened the gate of God's kingdom to the Gentiles. He cast the nets and caught many Jews, and he again cast the nets and caught many Gentiles. Yet subsequently, the nets—so far as what appeared outwardly before men —were broken, the kingdom was rejected, and the fish leaked out. Whereupon God called John to mend the nets, that is to say, to restore to the original condition.

Let us next see what God had in mind when Paul was called. At that time Paul was full of plans to persecute the believers. On the road to Damascus, God's light shone on him. And he asked, "What shall I do, Lord?" (Acts 22.10) So that his work is more a matter of "how to do it." Unlike Peter who in one day led three thousand to Christ, Paul was used in his ministry to win one person here, two persons there, and even tens of people elsewhere to the Lord, but not thousands. For Paul's primary task was not to draw people in but to build people up. The characteristic of his work was what should be done to the materials once they have been collected, how should the house be built, and how should the inside be arranged and set in order. And thus we find that his earthly occupation, which exemplified all this, was the making of tents for people to dwell in. So that in the spiritual realm, it could also be said that he made tents. Unlike Peter who only drew in a sheet, Paul was involved in making the sheet into a tent.

What was the general attitude of the people towards the works of these three men? Alas, it was very bad, for which we cannot help but sigh in sorrow. As we look into the situation of these three at the end of their ministries, we see that their testimonies are being rejected.

It is clearly shown, for example, in the Letter of Second Peter. By the time of its second chapter, false prophets have already come in, who specialize in counterfeiting work. There Peter labels them as dogs and swine, because they corrupt things so much as to confuse the kingdom of God. In the third chapter, mockers are mentioned. They are those who despise what Peter preaches and deem it shameful and detestable. In short, the testimony of the kingdom is totally rejected. In fact, Peter has been compelled to write this second letter because his first letter has been rejected and cast aside. And what is written in the second letter reveals the very last condition surrounding his testimony. He openly discloses how his testimony is being rejected by men.

Now if Peter's time was marked by such a declining state of affairs, how much more will this be true in our twentieth century! Rarely do we find people today who bear the testimony of the kingdom and who are not opposed or considered foolish for proclaiming it. No wonder there are so many who advocate a utopian ideal, as was the case in Peter's day. Who then ought to be surprised at the rampage of falsified truth, for all these things have previously occurred in Peter's time. Need we therefore be puzzled or bewildered by it in our time?

Yet this was not only the situation at the end of Peter's ministry; for does not Paul suffer the same fate? The last extant letter of his included in the New Testament is the Second Letter to Timothy. And not long afterwards Paul died. Thus in this last letter of his we can detect the clear outlines of Paul's final situation. At one point he wrote this: "*All* that are in Asia turned away from me" (2 Tim. 1.15). The current conditions then for anyone to manifest the Lord are too hard and too restrictive; many believers cannot endure them. Because they find them impossible, they turn back. Neither the apostle nor even the Lord himself could persuade them to stay and stick it out. Therefore the Lord and Paul must sadly let them go.

The Letter to the Philippians was also written by Paul in his advanced age. What there did he say? He said this: "All seek their own" (2.21). People once again are found casting aside the testimony of this apostle. So very important were their own affairs that they laid aside the Lord's interests. Yet if we attend to our own interests, how can we attend to the Lord's? We can only leave the Lord's concerns alone. So that once more the testimony of Paul is rejected and hated of men. His last word, therefore, is to exhort believers to be watchful and to be vigilant in guarding against the intrusion of heresies. And thus ends the ministry of Paul.

As a result, at the time when Paul and Peter died, the church in *outward appearance* had fallen into great spiritual declension, into the situations not unlike those described in Revelation chapters 2 and 3. The outward appearance of the testimony seems to indicate an almost total failure. Hence the Lord now begins to use John. What is he called to do? None other than to emphasize the inward work.

In this connection, have you noticed the kind of Gospel John wrote? Unlike Matthew who is strong on history, this apostle mainly records our relationship with God as that of a father-to-son relationship. His introduction or prologue does not, as is the case with Luke's Gospel, begin with Adam; nor does it begin with Abraham, as is true with Matthew's Gospel. Instead, John's Gospel opens up with Jesus Christ; he commences from the very, very Beginning. This is because outwardly speaking everything has failed; neither Adam nor Abraham can be restored; so that now it requires a going back to the *very* Beginning. And who or what is able to shake the Beginning? None, for the Beginning is unshakable. All that is of God is eternally unshakable. The Gospel according to John is none other than the record of the Word who is from the beginning and who has been expressed in order to lead us back to the design of the beginning.

What things are identified with the Beginning? They are life, light, and love. And these things are unshakable since they are *inward* realities. John in his Gospel has not addressed himself to external matters such as husband and wife, master and servant, or even Christian meetings. What he mentions are exclusively matters pertaining to God and that are absolutely internal in nature.

Due to the fact that today everything has failed and that the church in her outward appearance is already in ruin and is divided, we must ask God for grace that we may especially return to the ministry of John. Otherwise, all will be vain. This does not suggest that the works of Peter and Paul are unnecessary and no longer valid. It simply means that the urgent need of today lies not in outward things. Quite the contrary, there must first be inward reality and then we can again have these outward things. Let us acknowledge that the nets have already been broken, the fishes have been leaking out, and that God is calling for the ministry of John to mend the nets. And what he by mending adds on is not something new like some new discovery, but is simply that which has been there originally from the very beginning. Hence John writes elsewhere in this manner: "I have not written unto you because ye know not the truth, but because ye know it" (1 John 2.21)—that is to say, the problem is not because we do not know but because we know and have forgotten!

What is meant by mending? Mending is not the changing to new nets but is the restoring of the broken nets to their original condition. In other words, it is the filling up of the gap that has occurred with that which was from the beginning. The urgent need of this hour is for God's people to return to the Lord for life and spiritual power so as to overcome the world and the enemy. This is spiritual reality. And such must be grasped first before we can return to the testimonies of Paul and Peter. If we do not return to John first, we will not be able to return to Paul and then to Peter. Let me repeat that the nets have already been broken: and if that is true, then how can we ever catch the fish? Let the nets be mended first—let us first grasp that which is real—before we do anything else.

Finally, three Scripture verses deserve our special attention before concluding this discussion.

(1) "Another shall gird thee, and carry thee whither thou wouldest not" (John 21.18). This is the way the Lord Jesus foretold of Peter's end. Peter was such a strong and energetic person. For the sake of his Lord, he was crucified head downward, according to Christian tradition. How very brave he was. Yet what exactly did the Lord say about Peter? He said he would be brought by men to a place where he did not wish to go. From our vantage point some nineteen centuries later we see that he has been brought into the Roman Catholic system to be a "Father" of the "church." He has been made to sit on a throne in Rome. High above the cathedral that is there is inscribed in large letters St. Peter's Cathedral. Countless numbers of great men and lesser men praise him and carry him. But is Peter willing to be so treated? Unquestionably, he is most unwilling and unhappy about it. He never would have dreamed he would receive such glory today. He must find it extremely difficult to sit on such a high throne. But what can he possibly do? For is he not girded by other people and

carried in a direction he would never himself have chosen? Is not his freedom now fully manipulated by people and nations over whom he has no power? His testimony is completely buried! Oh how few there are who know that Peter is already bound.

People usually think that being saved is the happiest and most liberating experience. And I would hasten to say that salvation has indeed a most happy and liberating effect upon the redeemed ones; but the experience of being saved is not just for personal enjoyment and is certainly not for the opportunity of doing whatever we wish to do; on the contrary, it is to bring the Lord's people into subjection to the sovereignty of God. This alone is the right understanding of salvation as Peter presented it.

(2) Next, though, let us look at the ending of Paul. "He abode . . . in his own hired dwelling" (Acts 28.30). His ending was truly tragic. He had to live in a house he himself rented. Formerly Paul could live in Ephesus or even in Corinth, but now he had no permanent address: he did not even have his own house, but had to rent a place in which to live. In addition, Paul's testimony was rejected. With the result that he stayed in the house he rented and traveled abroad no more. Formerly Paul in great liberty would have come to your place to find you and to preach to you, but now you must go to his place or else you will not find him. Whether you believe in the truth or not, Paul has no way "to interfere" with you now. You must make your own decision. Paul has already been

overthrown by the great men in power. They have imprisoned him in Rome. And unless you go and seek him out, you will never see his face.

Today many people know only how to read the Lord's prayer and the creeds of their denominations. They live in their own houses. They do not visit Paul's dwelling. How totally inadequate it is to have only the mint and the anise (cf. Matt. 23.23). We must seek to find the real meaning of Paul's letters. For the Letters to the Corinthians were not just for the Corinthian saints; they are also for the entire church of God. But now Paul is being hidden away by men. He is not able to come forth and meet us. Let us therefore find him with eagerness, discover the real meaning of his testimony, and allow nothing to slip away. In utter frankness I would speak this word: that those who are unwilling to apply themselves earnestly shall never see Paul nor understand his testimony; all who fail to pay the cost shall never find the truth.

And finally, (3), let us consider John's end. "I John . . . was in the isle that is called Patmos" (Rev. 1.9). John was exiled to an island. What is an island? An island is different from the mainland as well as from the sea. It *is* in the sea and yet it is not of the sea: it stands by itself alone in the sea. It *is* land, and yet is not of the continent but disconnected from it. Hence we may say that an island is separated not only from the sea but also from the land. It is a most solitary place. What does the sea typify? It typifies the world. And the land? It stands for the religious organization of men, for the highest achievement of men is still but a continent. Spiritually speaking, then, an island is not joined to either of these two entities: neither to the world nor to religion. God too is not in the world system, nor is He in the gigantic human religious organization. And God wisely put His apostle on an island: John is neither in the world system nor in the religious system, but is in the island. And how solitary he must be. He enjoys neither the wave-like pleasures of the world nor the secure peace of religious institutional life. He is indeed most lonesome.

Yet a marvelous thing happens there on that isolated island. John is in the Spirit on the Lord's day; he sees a great vision; he hears the voice of the Lord Jesus; and he also is raptured to heaven. How beautiful all this is! Though there is not the pleasure of the sea nor the peace of the land, nevertheless, how sufficient it is to have the consolation of the Lord. Only those who are separated from both the sea and the land can enjoy union with the Lord. A Christian who is not willing to forsake position and fame in religion will never go to an island.

Do let us see that the Lord is calling us to the island. He wants us to forsake willingly all that is merely external and to draw nigh to Him. Although there is no boat in the sea nor bridge from the land, the Holy Spirit can carry us to the island. But as long as there are other conveniences, people will never go to the island.

To John we must therefore first return. Let us stand first on this reality, then return to the works of

Paul and Peter. Let us learn how to live on the island, how to dwell in the rented house, and how to be faithful though bound. May the Lord bless us all.

6 | The End of This Age and the Kingdom

We firmly believe that in our day we are nearing the end of this age. Moreover, we are aware of the fact that following this age of the church there is to be the age of the kingdom. The eyes of God have already turned towards the kingdom, which is increasingly receiving His attention. For if our understanding is correct we strongly believe that what God is anxious to bring in, according to His eternal will, is the kingdom. God's call upon the church is for the sake of the kingdom.

When the servant of the Lord catches a vision of the place the kingdom has in the predestinated will of God, how he then yearns for the soon coming of the kingdom. How he longs for all the children of God to cooperate with the Lord in hastening the arrival of the kingdom. The Bible verse which is especially impressed upon that servant's heart is more than likely Matthew 24.14, which says: "And this gospel of the kingdom shall be preached in the whole world for a testimony unto all the nations; and then shall the end come."

Here we may discern the relationship between the preaching of the gospel of the kingdom and the coming of the end. Unquestionably this verse is difficult to be understood clearly. In fact, in the past this verse has become an issue causing much contention among God's children. We ourselves have no intention to join in the arguments, for no matter how one may interpret this passage, it will not bring in a unanimous opinion among His people. We simply wish to present the light on this verse which we have received.

"The end of the age" (see Matt. 24.3 mg.) is a phrase which naturally points to the end of *this* age. According to a strict interpretation of prophecy, this phrase refers to "the hour of trial" (Rev. 3.10)—the latter also being understood as constituting the short period known as "the Great Tribulation" that will conclude the age in which we now live. Our age is variously termed the age of the Holy Spirit, the age of the church, the dispensation of grace, or the dispensation of the gospel. This age, which bears all these different titles, shall be terminated with the coming of "the end" or the Great Tribulation.

Now we must clearly recognize that the church is responsible to work with God in bringing in the kingdom, as Matthew 24.14 confirms. And in understanding that the kingdom of God can only appear publicly after the end of this age, the church cannot but be interested in the end itself. For though the end of this age has nothing to do with the church herself, it has much to do with the work of the church.

For this reason, the Lord Jesus tells us in Matthew 24.14 that the gospel of the kingdom must first be preached and then the kingdom of the heavens shall come. Here our Lord prophesies concerning the phenomena which shall occur at the approaching end of this age and the soon coming of the kingdom of the heavens. He in addition sets forth the condition for there to be the closing of this age and the introduction of the kingdom. So that from this verse in Matthew we see that for this age to be terminated, the children of God must bear witness to the gospel of the kingdom anew. At the time of the end of this age, we shall truly witness a revival of the gospel of the kingdom.

During the last several decades there seems to have been a gradual recovering of the teaching of the kingdom. Especially in the past few years the Lord has been turning the eyes of His children in China more towards this matter of the kingdom of God. This is indeed a very healthy sign.

But what *is* the kingdom of God? What is the gospel of the kingdom of the heavens? What is commonly understood is that the kingdom is the age when Christ and the church shall reign. Actually, it is much more than this.

Many try to differentiate between the gospel of the kingdom and the gospel of grace. This is really not necessary. If those in our audience insist on distinguishing them, then may we say that the gospel of grace deals principally with blessing while the gospel of the kingdom is especially directed against the demonic oppression of Satan.

Nowadays there are so many concepts about the

kingdom, but let us hear what the Lord Jesus has to say: "If I by the Spirit of God cast out demons, then is the kingdom of God come upon you" (Matt. 12.28). No doubt the kingdom means many things, but what the Lord mentions here may be deemed the most important meaning.

The kingdom is in direct opposition to Hades. The Lord Jesus declares that the kingdom is the casting out of demons—that is to say, that by the energy of the Spirit of God there is the casting out of demons. This is an accurate explanation of the kingdom. There is one basic lack to be found in today's Bible commentaries, in that their authors usually forget about Hades. The church in its position, work, thought, and speech has generally forgotten her enemy Satan. Know we not that God has chosen the church to *resist Satan* and to *bring in His kingdom*? For let us take note that the very first time the New Testament mentions the church it also mentions Hades (see Matt. 16).

We all know that the duration of the age of the kingdom is one thousand years. But what is the connection between this thousand years and Satan? In the opening verses of Revelation 20 we are told that this will be the time when Satan himself shall be chained in the abyss. This is the most shameful time for him.

"Know ye not that we shall judge angels?" (1 Cor. 6.3a) Now only those who have sinned need to be judged, and therefore we see from this verse that the future for the church will include the judging of the sinful angels. These sinful angels rebelled, along with Satan, against God. They are the principalities and powers of today (cf. Eph. 6.12, Col. 2.15), the princes mentioned in Daniel (10.13,20). And God says that we shall judge them. But when? At the time when Christ shall come again to set up His kingdom.

This then is the kingdom—the time when Satan is bound in the abyss. It is the time when all the principalities and powers shall be judged. Oh, the powers of Hades are to be destroyed in the kingdom time! And the beast as the son to Satan, and the spirit who is the false prophet, shall be cast into the lake of fire. Moreover, other countless evil spirits shall be driven away from the world and imprisoned. Satan himself shall be put to shame openly and pass a thousand years of life in darkness in the abyss. It is the time when he and his entire household of evil shall be completely defeated and destroyed. During this same period, the children of God are to be vindicated and the battle of the cross of Christ is to gain complete victory. This is the time when the purpose of God purposed from the ages against Satan finds its complete fulfillment. And what is prophesied in Isaiah 14 (verses 12–20), which is a veiled reference to Satan, is then totally realized. In the kingdom age, Satan shall have no influence at all.

Consequently, the preaching of the gospel of the kingdom of the heavens is nothing less than to declare that God who rules in heaven today shall tomorrow rule the earth by casting out completely the prince of today's world with all his followers and evil spirits so that the new man (Christ and His church) shall reign instead.

The gospel of the kingdom of the heavens is thus directed against the powers of darkness. So that when the Lord Jesus first proclaimed this gospel, all His works dealt with the powers of darkness: "To this end was the Son of God manifested, that he might destroy the works of the devil" (1 John 3.8). He both healed the sick and cast out demons. Now it is quite obvious to us that casting out demons is a work that destroys the kingdom of darkness. But how about the healing of the sick? The apostle Peter provides us with an explanation when, in describing Jesus' earthly ministry, he noted that our Lord went about "healing all that were oppressed of the devil" (Acts 10.38). If we read the Gospels carefully we shall observe that the entire earthly life of our Lord Jesus was set to destroy the work of the devil. Consequently, His work on earth had far greater effect on demons than on men.

Now the Lord Jesus tells us that at the end of this age His children will rise up to bear a similar testimony. We must thank the Lord for the fact that in very recent years not a few among the children of God have been raised up to battle with Satan. Spiritual warfare in the lives of many believers has become a reality, it no longer being merely a matter of terminology.

In order for the kingdom of God to come, in order for God's sovereignty to be manifested in the world and for Satan and his powers to be cast out, we must stand up to bear witness concerning the gospel of the kingdom of the heavens. In other words, we ought to testify to the victory of the cross of Christ. We should declare that Christ has already judged the prince of this world, that He has gained a total victory, and that the kingdom and glory and power are now entirely His. For Satan has no place in this age; he is merely usurping this time. Everyone who has received the Lord Jesus has been delivered from the power of darkness and been transferred to the kingdom of the Son of God's love (Col. 1.13). We must proclaim the gospel of the kingdom of the heavens—which is the gospel of the casting out of demons, the gospel of announcing the defeat of Satan and the destruction of Hades. And such testimony will bring this age to its end.

Admittedly, this age *is* the church age, for the church had her commencement in this age. At the same time, however, let us be aware that the Bible equally calls this age "an evil and adulterous generation" (Matt. 12.39), a "faithless and perverse generation" (Matt. 17.17), and "a crooked and perverse generation" (Phil. 2.15). The purpose of God is to bring such a generation and age to an end. He is pleased to see that the end of this age is coming soon so that His kingdom may be ushered in. But the children of God have their duty to perform. They should work together with God to bring this age to its end. Prayer is one of the ways, but testimony is also required. Let us all stand up for the "majesty" of the Lord Jesus as never before. Let us testify to His "government" more than ever. Although the kingdom of the Antichrist must precede the kingdom of

Christ, nevertheless we must testify to the kingdom of Christ before the coming of the kingdom of the Antichrist. We need to bring this age to its end.

Naturally this is not a new gospel, it is only that aspect of the one gospel which has for far too long been neglected by the church. Yet all the apostles had proclaimed this aspect of the gospel. Both Acts 14.22 and 28.23 bear witness to this fact: "Confirming the souls of the disciples, exhorting them to continue in the faith, and that through many tribulations we must enter into the kingdom of God"—"And when they had appointed him a day, they came to him into his lodging in great number; to whom he expounded the matter, testifying the kingdom of God, and persuading them concerning Jesus, both from the law of Moses and from the prophets, from morning till evening." Furthermore, after His resurrection the Lord Jesus himself spoke to His disciples the things concerning the kingdom of God (Acts 1.3). If we want to continue the work of the apostles we must testify to what they testified. How greatly the church has forgotten the victory, the authority, and the throne of Christ. Whoever dares to testify that "Christ alone is King; Satan is not" is really preaching the gospel of the kingdom of the heavens.

Let us not be people who are behind the times. Today there is but one gospel that is relevant to our times—namely, the gospel of the kingdom of Christ. By this we are not suggesting that we should preach nothing else; we only wish to underline the fact that God desires us to pay special attention to this aspect of the gospel. We must rise up and affirm what God has determined for this age. What He is interested in at the end of this age is the victory of His Son and the exile of Satan. If we are not of one mind with God on this matter, that is to say, if we do not pay attention to what He is now attending to, we will not accomplish the eternal will of God no matter what great work we may do. How far away we are from God's best if that be the case.

Today's need is for Christians who know the time. God is looking for a people who sympathize with Him and work with Him in concluding this age and ushering in the next. If Christians view as their greatest responsibility on earth the saving of people for their souls, then they have failed to accomplish the highest will of God. They ought to realize that they have a responsibility even greater than the saving of souls: that they are to bring this age to an end and bring in the kingdom of God. Their highest responsibility is to witness the destruction of God's archenemy Satan and all his powers of darkness. They ought to view this as the chief objective of all their works. Prayer is not just to pray, but to hurt Satan. Saving souls is not merely to save people, but to damage Satan in the process. Please do not misunderstand here. We do not demean the work of evangelism, for the saving of men and women is a most glorious task which we should never despise; but in the work of saving souls let us not lose sight of the kingdom. We will become most effective workers in the Lord's hand if we always keep in view the kingdom of God and the things regarding the determinate counsel of God and the settled destiny of God's enemy.

Why will it be that after the Lord's children testify to the kingdom of the heavens the end shall arrive? Here we may perceive again the working together of God and men. God desires the end to come. Yet if His children fail to work with Him in opposing this age and in desiring His kingdom to come, He will postpone the kingdom's arrival. But when God's children really abhor the sickening phenomena of this closing age and pray for its quick demise as well as pray for the kingdom, He will rise up and work. Whenever God's children rise up to bear the testimony of the kingdom of the heavens—which means they want what He wants and they hate what He hates at that time—their will is joined to the will of God. And this enables the Lord to rise up and work.

Let us never assume that the end will arrive automatically. No, if we do not desire God's will, His will shall be hindered. Hence God is waiting patiently today, seeking for those who are of one mind with Him and are willing to work together with Him in bringing in the end of this age. Who among us is willing to do this great work? Who among us is willing to pay the cost?

TITLES YOU
WILL WANT TO HAVE

By Watchman Nee

CD ROM – Complete works of Nee by CFP

Basic Lesson Series
Volume 1 – A Living Sacrifice
Volume 2 – The Good Confession
Volume 3 – Assembling Together
Volume 4- Not I, But Christ
Volume 5 – Do All to the Glory of God
Volume 6 – Love One Another

The Church and the Work
Volume 1 – Assembly Life
Volume 2 – Rethinking the Work
Volume 3 – Church Affairs
Revive Thy Work
The Word of the Cross
The Communion of the Holy Spirit
The Finest of the Wheat – Volume 1
The Finest of the Wheat – Volume 2
Take Heed
Worship God
Interpreting Matthew
The Character of God's Workman
Gleanings in the Fields of Boaz
The Spirit of the Gospel
The life That Wins
From Glory to Glory
The Spirit of Judgment
From Faith to Faith
Back to the Cross
The Lord My Portion
Aids to "Revelation"
Grace for Grace
The Better Covenant
A Balanced Christian Life
The Mystery of Creation

The Messenger of the Cross
Full of Grace and Truth – Volume 1
Full of Grace and Truth – Volume 2
The Spirit of Wisdom and Revelation
Whom Shall I Send?
The Testimony of God
The Salvation of the Soul
The King and the Kingdom of Heaven
The Body of Christ: A Reality
Let Us Pray
God's Plan and the Overcomers
The Glory of His Life
"Come, Lord Jesus"
Practical Issues of This Life
Gospel Dialogue
God's Work
Ye Search the Scriptures
The Prayer Ministry of the Church
Christ the Sum of All Spiritual Things
Spiritual Knowledge
The Latent Power of the Soul
The Ministry of God's Word
Spiritual Reality or Obsession
The Spiritual Man
The Release of The Spirit
Spiritual Authority

By Stephen Kaung

Discipled to Christ
The Splendor of His Ways
Seeing the Lord's End in Job
The Songs of Degrees
Meditations on Fifteen Psalms

ORDER FROM:

**Christian Fellowship Publishers, Inc.
11515 Allecingie Parkway
Richmond, Virginia 23235**